AF438662

The Art of Pendulum Healing:

Techniques, Tools, and Protection for Energy Work

The Art Of Pendulum Healing:

Techniques, Tools and Protection for Energy Work

Shani Riviere

Table Of Contents

Chapter 1: Introduction to Pendulums

What Pendulums Are and Their Historical Significance in Healing Practices

Pendulums are simple yet powerful tools that have been used for centuries across cultures for various forms of spiritual and energetic work. Typically consisting of a weighted object attached to a string or chain, a pendulum responds to subtle energy fields by swinging in different directions or patterns. This movement is thought to connect us with our inner guidance, higher consciousness, or unseen energies, allowing us to access answers to questions and insights into our well-being.

The roots of pendulum use trace back thousands of years. Ancient Egyptians, Chinese, and Europeans used pendulums and similar tools for divination, dowsing, and healing. In medieval Europe, pendulums were often used to locate underground water sources, a practice that evolved into modern dowsing. Over time, people noticed pendulums' responsiveness to other forms of energy as well, such as emotional or physical imbalances within the human body. In ancient Chinese culture, pendulum-like movements were observed in health and healing techniques, thought to enhance Qi flow and restore balance.

By the 20th century, pendulums gained a prominent role in spiritual healing and alternative medicine. Healers and energy practitioners began to use them to gauge the body's energy, uncover imbalances, and assist in clearing blocked or stagnant energies. The renewed interest in holistic and natural health practices has led to a resurgence in pendulum use, with people worldwide using pendulums to connect with their intuition, gain clarity on health concerns, and enhance their personal healing practices. The pendulum remains a popular tool among energy healers and individuals alike for its accessibility, ease of use, and remarkable ability to tap into the body's energy fields.

The Science and Energy Behind Pendulum Movement

Pendulum movement may seem mysterious, but it can be explained in part by the principles of physics and energy. At its core, a pendulum's movement relies on gravity and momentum, which is why when you set a pendulum in motion, it will swing in a consistent, predictable pattern. However, a unique quality of pendulums is their high sensitivity to subtle forces around them, including unseen energetic influences. This sensitivity is part of what makes pendulums valuable as tools for healing and spiritual guidance.

When you hold a pendulum, even the smallest muscle movements in your hand or fingers can influence its motion. These movements may be unconscious responses to your thoughts, emotions, or focused intentions, creating what appears to be an independent motion. This phenomenon, called the ideomotor effect, has been studied scientifically and describes how the mind and body interact to produce subtle movements. This means that when you focus on a question or healing intention, your body's micromovements can influence the pendulum in a meaningful way, creating a bridge between thought and action.

In addition to the ideomotor effect, the pendulum's movement is often interpreted by practitioners as a response to changes in the energy field surrounding it. According to energy healing theories, each person has an energetic aura or biofield that fluctuates based on health, emotions, and external influences. A pendulum is thought to respond to this biofield, with its movements representing an exchange of energy or information between the pendulum and the body's aura. While conventional science does not yet fully explain this interaction, energy healers believe that these subtle energies can influence a pendulum in ways beyond the physical.

Furthermore, the concept of resonance is significant in pendulum use. Resonance does occur when two objects vibrating at similar frequencies then amplify each other. When you use a pendulum with focused intention, it is thought that your intention resonates with the pendulum, creating a powerful feedback loop. This resonance between the pendulum and your own energy field allows the pendulum to act as a kind of conduit, amplifying subtle signals from your subconscious or energetic self into visible movements.

How Pendulums Connect to the Body's Energy Fields

The human body is more than just physical matter; it also encompasses a complex energy system, often referred to in holistic and Eastern medicine as the *aura*, *biofield*, or *energy field*. This energy field contains layers of subtle energies that interact with our physical and mental well-being. Within this field lie energy centers, or *chakras*, that regulate and distribute life force, often called *Qi* or *prana*. When these energies are balanced and flowing, our physical and emotional health tends to be stable. However, stress, trauma, and environmental factors can disrupt this flow, leading to imbalance or illness.

Pendulums can interact with this energy field by providing feedback about the condition of specific chakras or other areas within the body's biofield. Energy healers and practitioners often use pendulums to perform an "energy scan," in which they hold the pendulum over each chakra or area of the body, observing how it responds. For example, a pendulum held over the heart chakra may show a strong, clear swing if the energy is healthy, or it may spin erratically or not at all if the chakra is blocked or depleted. By observing these responses, practitioners can assess where energetic intervention may be beneficial.

To provide deeper insight, here are common interpretations of pendulum movement in relation to the body's energy:

- **Clockwise motion**: Often viewed as an indication of balanced, positive energy flow. It may show that the chakra or energy center is open and functioning properly.

- **Counterclockwise motion**: May suggest that the energy center is releasing or clearing, which can be beneficial if it has been holding onto negative energy. Some practitioners view this as a "cleansing" motion.
- **Back-and-forth swing**: Often interpreted as a neutral response, or a "yes" answer when asking questions. It can also indicate that the energy in that area is in balance.
- **Side-to-side swing**: This can be seen as an indication of imbalance or blockage in the energy center, or a "no" answer when asking questions.

Beyond simply reading energy, pendulums are also used to *influence* energy. During healing sessions, a practitioner might hold a pendulum over a blocked chakra with the intention of restoring its flow. The pendulum's vibrations are believed to resonate with the body's energy, gently nudging it back into balance. This technique is also used for grounding, where the pendulum is held close to the base of the spine or feet to stabilize and anchor a person's energy.

The pendulum's ability to interact with and adjust these energy fields makes it a versatile tool in energy healing, helping to identify imbalances and facilitate the body's natural healing process. By harnessing the pendulum's sensitivity to energy, we can develop a deeper awareness of our body's energetic state and cultivate self-healing practices that promote alignment and harmony.

Pendulums are more than objects—they are a bridge between the material world and the unseen realm of energy and intuition. By interpreting their movements, we gain access to insights that lie beyond the conscious mind, offering a way to understand and balance our own energy. With a pendulum, we have a tool that not only reveals the condition of our inner world but also aids in its transformation.

In the next chapters, we'll explore how to select the right pendulum for healing, learn to interpret its movements accurately, and build a personal practice that supports intuitive connection and energetic balance.

Chapter 2: Choosing the Right Pendulum

Types of Materials in Pendulums and Their Properties

Choosing a pendulum is a highly personal process, as each material has distinct energetic properties that influence the pendulum's effectiveness. Understanding the types of materials used in pendulums and their unique qualities can help you select one that aligns best with your healing goals and personal energy.

Crystal Pendulums

Crystals are one of the most popular materials for pendulums due to their natural energetic properties. Each crystal vibrates at a specific frequency, and these vibrations interact with the body's energy field in unique ways. Here are some commonly used crystals for pendulums and their properties:

- **Clear Quartz**: Known as the "master healer," clear quartz amplifies energy and intention, making it highly versatile for all types of healing work. It is excellent for those just starting with pendulum work because of its clear and direct energy.

- **Amethyst**: A crystal of spirituality and protection, amethyst is helpful for work involving emotional healing, intuitive insights, and spiritual growth. It is particularly effective for those using pendulums in meditation or for accessing higher levels of consciousness.

- **Rose Quartz**: Associated with love, compassion, and emotional healing, rose quartz is often chosen for heart-centered work. It is gentle and nurturing, making it ideal for self-care and relationships.

- **Black Obsidian**: Known for its grounding and protective qualities, black obsidian is useful for cleansing negative energy and staying centered during sessions. It is often used when there is a need for protection or to create a safe, grounded space for healing.

- **Tiger's Eye**: This stone is linked to inner strength, courage, and focus. It can help with issues related to self-confidence, decision-making, and personal empowerment, providing a sense of stability in the pendulum work.

- **Lapis Lazuli**: With strong links to communication and truth, lapis lazuli is beneficial for clarity and honesty. It helps bring forward hidden truths and encourages authenticity, making it a powerful tool for those using pendulums for guidance and insight.

Each crystal holds a specific vibration that can amplify the purpose of the pendulum work. Crystal pendulums are sensitive to energy fields and can be influenced by both the user's energy and the energy of the surrounding environment, making them ideal for work that requires a delicate touch and deep focus.

Metal Pendulums

Metal pendulums are known for their strong, consistent energy, which makes them suitable for users seeking precision and durability. Metals are conductive materials that can enhance energy flow, and each metal has its own energetic qualities. Here are some commonly used metals in pendulums and their properties:

- **Brass**: Known for its ability to conduct energy, brass is commonly used in pendulums for divination and dowsing. Its energy is grounding and stabilizing, which helps the user stay focused and calm during pendulum work.

- **Copper**: Copper is a highly conductive metal, often associated with the flow of energy and intuition. It is known to amplify energy and can be particularly effective in healing work, as it enhances the pendulum's connection to the energy fields.

- **Silver**: Silver is linked to the moon and the feminine, bringing a gentle, intuitive quality to the pendulum's energy. It is useful for emotional and intuitive work, as it resonates with subtle energies and can help deepen the user's connection to their inner guidance.

- **Gold**: Gold is a powerful conductor of energy and has a high vibrational frequency. It represents wealth, abundance, and vitality, and it is especially suited for high-level healing work. Gold pendulums are often used by advanced practitioners who seek to access higher frequencies of energy.

Metal pendulums are durable and retain their shape and form over time, making them an excellent choice for regular use. They provide a steady, grounded energy that can be particularly helpful for beginners, as their movements are often clearer and easier to interpret than those of crystal pendulums.

Wooden Pendulums

Wooden pendulums have a warm, natural energy and are often associated with grounding and connecting to the Earth's energy. Unlike crystal or metal pendulums, which conduct energy more intensely, wood has a gentler, more stabilizing influence. This makes wooden pendulums an excellent choice for those who want a grounded, calming presence in their healing work.

- **Oak**: Oak is strong and grounding, offering stability and protection. It is often chosen by those seeking to stay rooted and connected to the earth during pendulum work.

- **Maple**: Maple wood has a soft, nurturing energy and is often used for healing and introspective work. Its gentle vibration makes it suitable for emotional healing and balancing.

- **Pine**: Pine carries a refreshing, uplifting energy. It is helpful for those working with spiritual cleansing or energetic purification, as it aligns well with intentions to clear negative energies.

- **Cherry:** Cherry wood is known for its gentle warm energy often associated with love, joy and renewal. It can support work aimed at emotional healing, reconnecting with your inner peace and makes an excellent choice for beginners or those seeking to integrate compassion and gentleness into their practice. Useful in meditation and reflective practices.

- **African Blackwood:** Known for its protective and grounding properties. Often used by advanced practitioners who require steady and strong energy for deep focused work. Its energy is grounding and stabilizing and can help keep users centered during intense sessions or when working with strong potentially chaotic energies. Helpful in energy work that involves protection or removing blockages. African Blackwood pendulums can have a strong, precise swing making them a good choice for users who prefer clear, decisive movements from their pendulum.

- **Yew:** Yew wood is a deeply mystical and ancient wood associated with transformation, rebirth and spiritual insight. Yew trees were symbols of eternal life and mystery in ancient cultures and pendulums made from yew are thought to have strong connections to ancestral wisdom, making them suitable for work involving spiritual guidance, inner transformation and self discovery. They resonate particularly well with users focused on exploring deeper spiritual realms or those interested in past life work, intuitive exploration, or ancestral healing. Yew pendulums tend to have a more subtle but deeply resonant swing, which can draw the user into a meditative, reflective state.

Wooden pendulums are a good choice for users who prefer a natural, grounding connection during their sessions. Their movements may be subtler than those of crystal or metal pendulums, but they can provide deep insight and a calming influence, especially in grounding or meditative practices. By selecting a wood that aligns with your intentions, you can cultivate a deeper, more harmonious connection with your pendulum, amplifying the guidance it provides and strengthening your healing practice.

Resin Pendulums

Resin pendulums are relatively new but growing in popularity. Resin is a versatile material that can encapsulate other objects, like small crystals, herbs, or even metals. This allows users to personalize their pendulums to match their specific intentions. Resin itself is neutral, so it doesn't interfere with the energetic qualities of the items within it.

- **Crystal-Embedded Resin**: Resin pendulums with embedded crystals allow the user to combine the qualities of specific stones with the durability of resin. This combination provides the added benefits of the crystal without the brittleness that some stones may have.

- **Herbal Resin Pendulums**: Some resin pendulums are infused with herbs, which can add specific energetic qualities. For example, lavender resin pendulums are thought to encourage calmness, while sage-infused pendulums may aid in clearing energy.

Resin pendulums are durable and versatile, and they can serve as customizable tools that blend the energetic qualities of different materials. They are especially useful for practitioners who want to work with specific crystals, colors, or herbs in their pendulum practice.

Glass Pendulums

Glass pendulums are valued for their neutrality. Unlike crystals, which have specific energetic properties, glass is considered energetically neutral, allowing it to serve as a clear and unbiased medium for reading energy. Glass pendulums are often preferred for straightforward question-and-answer work, as they can deliver pure responses without being influenced by the qualities of specific stones or metals.

- **Clear Glass**: Clear glass pendulums are ideal for clarity and simplicity in readings. They don't carry the inherent qualities of other materials, so they are less likely to influence the results with their own energy.

- **Colored Glass**: Some glass pendulums are tinted to correspond with chakra colors (e.g., blue for the throat chakra, green for the heart chakra). This color association can enhance specific types of energy work, particularly when focusing on a particular chakra.

Glass pendulums are also lightweight and responsive, making them a good choice for those who need a quick, responsive tool. They are typically used for general divination and are particularly popular for straightforward "yes" or "no" questions.

Selecting the Right Material for Your Healing Intentions

The material of a pendulum does more than simply dictate its appearance or weight; it directly impacts the kind of energy the pendulum brings to a healing session. By carefully selecting a material that aligns with their healing objectives, practitioners can create a harmonious environment for their clients and enhance the session's effectiveness.

For example:

- For emotional healing or heart-centered work, **rose quartz or cherry wood** pendulums can foster compassion and emotional release.
- When seeking grounding and protection, **brass or African blackwood** pendulums provide stabilizing energy that can support both the practitioner and client.
- For work requiring energetic flow and balance, **copper pendulums** enhance the practitioner's ability to clear blockages and facilitate energy flow.

Understanding how different materials impact healing work allows practitioners to create more intentional, focused healing sessions that cater to the unique needs of each client.

Guide: Choosing a Pendulum That Resonates with Your Personal Energy

Selecting a pendulum that aligns with your personal energy is a meaningful process that combines intuition, self-awareness, and understanding of the unique properties of different materials. Since each pendulum carries its own frequency, your ideal choice will not only resonate with your goals but will also feel naturally attuned to your inner energy. This guide will take you through each step of choosing the right pendulum for your personal journey.

Step 1: Identify Your Purpose

Begin by considering what you plan to use your pendulum for, as this will guide your choice in materials and shapes. Pendulums can serve various purposes, including:

- **Healing** (emotional, physical, or spiritual),
- **Energy balancing** or **chakra work**,
- **Divination** and **intuitive guidance**, and
- **Personal meditation** or **spiritual growth**.

For example, if you intend to use the pendulum primarily for healing work, a crystal pendulum that aligns with specific energy centers may be beneficial. If grounding and protection are priorities, a pendulum made from a grounding material like brass or blackwood may serve you best.

Step 2: Choose the Material That Aligns with Your Energy and Intentions

Each material brings its own energy signature, so choose one that supports your purpose and resonates with your personal energy. Below are some popular options and their qualities:

Crystals:

- **Clear Quartz**: Amplifies energy and intention, making it suitable for any type of work.
- **Amethyst**: Connects to spiritual and emotional healing; ideal for calming energy and opening intuition.
- **Rose Quartz**: Resonates with love and compassion, excellent for heart-centered and emotional work.
- **Black Tourmaline or Obsidian**: Protective, grounding, and ideal for cleansing negative energy.

  Choose a crystal pendulum if you are drawn to natural stones, have an affinity for specific crystal properties, or feel that certain stones amplify your energy.

Metals:

- **Brass**: Grounding, durable, and helps with focus.
- **Copper**: Amplifies energy flow, excellent for healing and clearing blockages.
- **Silver**: Reflects intuitive energy, particularly effective for emotional work and connection to lunar energy.

Opt for a metal pendulum if you desire stability, grounding, and consistent energy flow.

Wood:

- **Oak**: Known for strength and resilience, grounding and protective.

- **Cherry Wood**: Warm and uplifting, suited for joy and self-love.
- **Yew**: Mystical, transformative, and ideal for spiritual exploration.

Wooden pendulums are great for those who seek a connection to natural, earthy energy and prefer a gentler influence in their practice.

Glass or Resin:

- **Glass**: Neutral and adaptable, suitable for simple and direct question-answer work.
- **Resin with embedded crystals or herbs**: Allows customization for specific healing intentions.

  Consider a glass or resin pendulum if you want a neutral tool that doesn't carry strong energetic qualities on its own.

Step 3: Hold and Test the Pendulum's Energy

Once you have selected a few pendulums based on material, take time to connect with each one individually. Here's how:

1. **Hold the Pendulum in Your Dominant Hand**: Close your eyes and take a few deep breaths. Feel its weight and texture. Does it feel comfortable and pleasant in your hand?

2. **Observe Your Physical and Emotional Response**: Notice how the pendulum's energy feels. Some may bring a sense of calm, while others might create a feeling of excitement or focus. Trust your initial reactions, as these often reflect how well the pendulum aligns with your energy.

3. **Perform a "Yes" and "No" Test**: Holding the pendulum over your palm, ask it to show you a "yes" response and then a "no" response. If the pendulum responds smoothly and with ease, it is likely attuned to your energy. If it feels sluggish or inconsistent, it may not be the right fit.

Step 4: Listen to Your Intuition

Your intuition is a powerful tool in selecting a pendulum. If a particular pendulum feels like it "calls" to you or you feel a strong pull toward it, this is often a sign that it resonates with your energy. Trust your gut instincts. Even if a pendulum isn't made from your "preferred" material, it could still be a perfect match for your personal frequency.

Some people find they are instantly drawn to a certain shape, color, or material. Allow this natural attraction to guide your decision-making. You'll often find that the pendulum you're intuitively drawn to will be the one that works best with you.

Step 5: Cleanse and Dedicate Your Pendulum

Once you've selected your pendulum, cleanse it to clear any residual energy from previous handling. You can do this by:

- **Smudging** with sage or palo santo,
- **Placing it under moonlight** (particularly during a full moon),
- **Submerging it briefly in saltwater** (check that the material is salt-safe),
- **Burying it in earth** overnight (ideal for grounding stones and woods).

After cleansing, take a moment to set your intentions. Hold your pendulum and, either silently or aloud, state your purpose for the pendulum. This could be something like, "I dedicate this pendulum for use in healing and clarity in my work," or simply, "I attune this pendulum to my highest intentions."

Dedicating the pendulum in this way creates an energetic connection, helping the pendulum align fully with your energy.

Additional Tips for Finding the Perfect Match

- **Allow Time and Patience**: Sometimes, finding the right pendulum may take time. Visit various stores, explore options, or even consider custom-made pendulums if you feel you need a unique combination of materials.

- **Check Your Energy Level**: You'll get clearer responses when you're calm, grounded, and centered. If you're feeling off or emotionally unsettled, wait until you're in a balanced state to choose your pendulum.
- **Keep an Open Mind**: Be open to trying different shapes and sizes. Some may find a smaller pendulum feels best, while others may prefer larger, more substantial pieces. Experimenting will help you discover what feels most natural.

Selecting a pendulum is a deeply personal experience, as it becomes an extension of your intuitive and energetic practice. Choosing one that resonates with your personal energy enhances its effectiveness, making your healing or divination work smoother and more rewarding. By following these steps and trusting your intuition, you'll find the pendulum that resonates harmoniously with your energy and amplifies your connection to the spiritual realm.

Chapter 3: How to Use a Pendulum

Pendulums are versatile tools that can be used for a wide variety of purposes, from dowsing for answers to facilitating energetic healing. Using a pendulum effectively, however, involves more than just holding it and asking questions; it requires building a connection, understanding the nuances of its movements, and developing a consistent practice.

In this chapter, we'll go through a step-by-step guide on holding and using your pendulum, techniques for building a bond with it, and interpreting the basic movements and swings to help you make the most of your pendulum work.

Part 1: Step-by-Step Guide to Holding and Using a Pendulum

Before you begin working with your pendulum, ensure you are in a calm, grounded state. It's important to be clear-minded and focused when using a pendulum, as your mental and emotional state can influence its movements.

Step 1: Set Your Intentions

Begin by setting a clear intention for your session. Whether you are seeking guidance, trying to answer a specific question, or performing an energy check-in, clarify your purpose so that your energy aligns with your intentions.

Step 2: Find a Comfortable Position

- **Sit comfortably** in a chair with your feet flat on the ground, or stand with a stable posture. If seated, place your elbows on a table, so your arm and wrist can remain steady.
- **Hold the pendulum in your dominant hand** by pinching the top of its chain or cord between your thumb and index finger, leaving about four to six inches of chain free for smooth movement.

Step 3: Stabilize Your Hand

To maintain steady control:

- Rest your elbow on a stable surface.
- Allow the pendulum to hang freely from your fingers, keeping your hand steady to avoid any unintentional influence on its movement.

Step 4: Ask for Clear Communication

Take a few moments to connect with your pendulum. Silently or aloud, ask it to communicate clearly. You might say, "I ask for clear and truthful guidance through this pendulum. Please show me yes, no, and other directional answers in alignment with my highest good."

Step 5: Establish Baseline Movements

It's essential to establish the basic responses of your pendulum. Ask it to show you specific answers:

1. **"Please show me Yes."** Observe how the pendulum swings. It might move in a specific direction—vertically, horizontally, or in a clockwise or counter-clockwise circle.

2. **"Please show me No."** Notice how it responds. Typically, it will swing in a different direction than "Yes."

3. **"Please show me Neutral."** This might be a still position or a slight back-and-forth movement.

Document these responses to establish a baseline. Every pendulum might respond differently, and knowing your pendulum's unique language is key to interpreting answers accurately.

Step 6: Begin Asking Questions

Once you've established the baseline movements:

- Ask clear, simple, yes-or-no questions. Avoid open-ended or complex questions, as these are harder to interpret.

- Observe the direction of the pendulum's swing and interpret the response based on your established baseline movements.

Techniques for Building a Bond with Your Pendulum

To get accurate and meaningful responses, it's helpful to build a bond with your pendulum. Developing this connection will enhance your intuition and create a more harmonious flow between you and the pendulum's energy.

Practice Daily Connection Exercises

Spend a few minutes each day holding or meditating with your pendulum. This practice strengthens your connection to the pendulum's energy, creating a clearer channel for communication.

1. **Meditate with Your Pendulum**: Hold the pendulum in your hand while meditating to become attuned to its energy. Allow yourself to feel its vibrations and sense its presence.
2. **Set Personal Intentions**: Dedicate your pendulum to specific intentions, such as healing, clarity, or spiritual guidance. This dedication reinforces your energy and purpose when you use it.

Engage in Simple Exercises to Strengthen the Bond

Building a rapport with your pendulum is similar to building trust in a relationship. The more you practice with it, the more responsive and accurate it becomes.

1. **"Yes" or "No" Games**: Start by asking it questions that you know the answers to, like, "Is my name [Your Name]?" This builds confidence in interpreting its responses.

2. **Emotion Check-Ins**: Ask the pendulum to show the energy surrounding your current emotional state. This helps establish a baseline for how your energy influences the pendulum's movement.

3. **Daily Energy Alignment**: Before starting a session, ask the pendulum, "Am I in the right energetic state for this session?" If it swings "no," take a few minutes to ground and center yourself.

Cleanse and Recharge Your Pendulum

Cleansing your pendulum regularly clears any residual or unwanted energy it may have absorbed. You can cleanse it by:

- **Smudging with sage or palo santo**,
- **Placing it under moonlight**, especially during a full moon,
- **Submerging it briefly in saltwater** (only if the material is salt-safe), or
- **Burying it in soil** overnight for grounding. Cleansing is especially important if your pendulum feels unresponsive or if you've used it for intense healing work.

Interpreting Basic Movements and Directional Swings

Once you've built a bond with your pendulum and established baseline responses, you're ready to interpret its movements in greater detail. Pendulum responses can provide guidance on simple yes-or-no questions, energetic readings, and even subtle cues about emotional or spiritual conditions.

Common Pendulum Movements and Their Meanings

1. **Vertical Swings**: Often represent a "Yes" response, but this can vary. Ensure it aligns with your baseline.
2. **Horizontal Swings**: Commonly signify "No" and can also indicate resistance to a question.
3. **Clockwise Circles**: Typically indicate positive energy or affirmation. They're often used in healing to confirm balanced or beneficial energy.
4. **Counterclockwise Circles**: Often suggest negative energy or caution. This swing might indicate an imbalance, blockage, or the need for grounding.

Interpreting Additional Movements

In addition to basic yes-or-no answers, pendulum movements can reveal other insights.

1. **Swinging in a Diagonal Line**: This can suggest a "Maybe" or "Uncertain" response, often meaning that conditions are not fully set, or additional information is needed.

2. **Erratic Movements**: If the pendulum's movements are irregular or erratic, it might be sensing chaotic energy or interference. Take a moment to ground yourself, cleanse the pendulum, and reset your energy before continuing.

3. **Stillness or Little Movement**: If your pendulum is unusually still, it could indicate that you're not in an ideal state to use it, or it may not be receiving a clear signal. Take a break, ground yourself, or come back to the question later.

Using the Pendulum for Chakra and Energy Work

Pendulums are often used to check for blockages or imbalances in the body's energy centers, or chakras:

1. **Hover the Pendulum Over Each Chakra**: Hold the pendulum about an inch above each chakra point, beginning at the root and moving up to the crown.

2. **Observe Its Movements**: If the pendulum swings strongly in a clockwise motion, this generally indicates a balanced chakra. A counterclockwise swing or no movement at all can signal an imbalance or blockage in that energy center.

This type of energy check-in can reveal physical or emotional areas needing attention and support.

Responding to Pendulum Answers and Adjusting Your Approach

It's essential to approach your pendulum's responses with an open mind. A pendulum is a tool that reflects your inner wisdom and energy, so if an answer feels unclear or challenging, pause and reflect on your question. Sometimes rephrasing or adjusting your approach can help. Over time, your confidence will grow, and you'll interpret responses with greater ease and accuracy.

Using a pendulum is a rewarding journey that deepens over time with practice, patience, and trust. As you continue working with your pendulum, it will become an extension of your intuitive self, bringing clarity, alignment, and insight to your healing and divination practices. Each session is an opportunity to refine your connection, enhance your focus, and build a reliable bond that strengthens your self-awareness and spiritual growth.

Chapter 4: Techniques for Healing with Pendulums

Healing with pendulums is an ancient and profound practice that utilizes the pendulum's energetic properties to identify, align, and harmonize different aspects of our energy field. By understanding and applying specific techniques, a practitioner can work with the pendulum to clear blockages, balance chakras, and restore physical, mental, and emotional well-being.

In this chapter, we'll cover three main techniques for pendulum healing: aligning chakras, clearing blockages in the energy field, and balancing physical, mental, and emotional energies. We'll also include two personal stories that illustrate the transformative power of these techniques in real-life applications.

Aligning Chakras Using Pendulum Energy

Understanding Chakra Alignment

The body has seven main chakras, or energy centers, that each correspond to different physical, emotional, and spiritual attributes. When these chakras are balanced and aligned, energy flows smoothly through the body, supporting health and well-being. However, when one or more chakras are out of alignment, it can lead to emotional distress, physical ailments, or even spiritual imbalance. Using a pendulum to assess and align chakras is a powerful way to restore this natural energy flow.

Step-by-Step Guide for Chakra Alignment

Preparation and Grounding

- Begin by centering yourself in a calm and grounded state. Take a few deep breaths, visualize your energy rooting down into the earth, and set an intention for healing.
- Hold your pendulum, allowing it to rest until it's completely still. Make sure you've cleansed it beforehand to ensure clarity in your readings.

Assess Each Chakra's Energy

- Start at the root chakra (located at the base of the spine) and work your way up to the crown chakra (top of the head).
- Hover the pendulum about an inch above each chakra point and allow it to move naturally. Observe the direction, strength, and speed of its swing.
  - **Clockwise Movement**: Typically indicates balanced energy.
  - **Counterclockwise Movement**: Often suggests blocked or stagnant energy.
  - **Stillness or Minimal Movement**: May indicate an energy blockage or disconnect in that chakra.

Balance the Chakra

- If you observe any imbalance, use your intention and visualization techniques to invite healing energy to that area.
- For example, if the pendulum swings counterclockwise over the solar plexus chakra, visualize a bright, golden light at the center of this chakra, expanding outward to restore its energy.
- Ask the pendulum to assist in clearing and balancing this chakra. Hold it above the chakra and visualize the pendulum drawing in healing energy, encouraging it to swing clockwise.

Repeat for Each Chakra

Move through each chakra in succession. As you balance each one, note any shifts or sensations in your body. Some people feel tingling or warmth as the chakras realign, indicating energy flow restoration.

Finish with Grounding

After aligning all chakras, visualize grounding energy flowing through your body, down into the earth. This step reinforces the alignment and helps you feel stable and balanced after the session.

o

Personal Story: Chakra Healing with the Heart

One client I worked with, Paulette, was experiencing emotional challenges following a recent breakup. During a chakra alignment session, her pendulum indicated an imbalance in her heart chakra by swinging erratically. As I guided her through a visualization of green healing light (associated with the heart chakra), the pendulum gradually shifted into a clockwise motion, signaling alignment. After the session, Sarah reported feeling more peaceful and open to healing, a process that continued as she worked with the pendulum over several weeks to maintain her heart chakra's balance.

Clearing Blockages in the Energy Field

The Purpose of Energy Clearing

Throughout daily life, we encounter various stresses, negative interactions, and environments that can impact our energy field. Over time, this can lead to energy blockages, which feel like stagnant or heavy areas in our aura. These blockages may manifest as fatigue, stress, or emotional discomfort. Pendulums can help identify and clear these blockages, creating a sense of release and revitalization.

Step-by-Step Guide to Clearing Blockages

Identify the Blockage Area

- Begin by scanning the body with the pendulum, similar to the chakra alignment process. However, in this case, focus on any part of the energy field that feels heavy or unbalanced.

- Pay attention to sensations in your hands or any unexpected movements in the pendulum, as these can be indicators of energy blockage.

Assess the Blockage's Nature

- If the pendulum swings in a chaotic or counterclockwise motion, this could indicate an area with energetic stagnation. Trust your intuition about the quality of energy present.
- Use this moment to tune into any thoughts, images, or feelings that arise. Sometimes blockages relate to specific emotional issues or past experiences.

Set the Intention to Clear

- Visualize the pendulum as a channel for clearing energy. Hold it over the blocked area, and imagine a gentle, healing light flushing away the stagnant energy. You may visualize the pendulum sweeping the blockage away as it swings.
- Allow the pendulum to continue moving until it naturally comes to a still point. Often, the pendulum will start swinging clockwise on its own, indicating a shift toward clearer energy.

Ground and Close the Session

After clearing the energy, perform a grounding exercise to solidify the change. You can visualize roots extending from your feet or a grounding light entering through the crown chakra and moving downwards.

A client, Aleks, approached me with complaints of chronic stress and anxiety. During our session, I noticed the pendulum moved erratically around his solar plexus area, a typical site for stress and self-worth issues. As I guided James through calming breathwork, I used the pendulum to sweep his solar plexus, setting an intention to clear the blockage. The pendulum gradually shifted to a clockwise swing, indicating that the energy was becoming clear. AleAleks felt an immediate sense of calm and described the session as "releasing a weight he didn't know he was carrying."

Using Pendulums to Balance Physical, Mental, and Emotional Energy

Physical Healing with Pendulums

Pendulums can support physical healing by helping to locate areas of stagnation or tension in the body and by directing positive energy to those areas.

1. **Identify the Physical Discomfort**: Hold the pendulum over the area of discomfort or ask it to help reveal areas needing healing.
2. **Encourage Positive Energy Flow**: As the pendulum swings, visualize healing light entering the area, gradually alleviating tension or pain.
3. **Track Progress**: Periodically use the pendulum to gauge progress in healing. The movement may become stronger as physical health improves.

Mental and Emotional Balancing

Pendulums can also bring insight into our mental and emotional state, helping us identify areas where we may need clarity or release.

1. **Mental Clarity**: When mental energy feels scattered, use the pendulum to identify areas of your body that may be holding onto stress.
2. **Emotional Healing**: For emotional balancing, begin with the heart or sacral chakra. Hold the pendulum over these areas and allow it to guide you toward feelings that need to be processed. Emotions such as sadness, anger, or frustration may manifest as heavy pendulum swings or counterclockwise motions.
3. **Reinforce Positivity**: Once you feel a shift, use the pendulum to bring in positive energy by focusing on affirmations or visualizing peaceful imagery.

Practical Example: Balancing Emotions with Pendulum Energy

During a time of personal transition, I felt my emotions were all over the place. In one session, I used my pendulum over my sacral and heart chakras to assess any imbalances. I noticed a counterclockwise swing over my heart, a sign that grief or sadness might be affecting me. After acknowledging these emotions, I used the pendulum to bring in calming energy, visualizing peace and stability. This practice helped me process and release emotions, allowing me to return to a balanced emotional state over time.

Pendulum healing can create profound transformations by aligning our physical, mental, and emotional energies. Through consistent practice, you can deepen your understanding of how your energy flows and use pendulum healing to support yourself and others on a path to holistic wellness. Each healing session brings greater awareness and balance, strengthening the connection between the pendulum and your inner energy field.

Chapter 5: Protective Measures When Using Pendulums

Using a pendulum for healing and divination connects you to various energies, and while this can be deeply enlightening, it's essential to establish protective practices to ensure a safe and effective experience. Grounding yourself, cleansing your pendulum, and creating energetic shields are key protective steps that help maintain clarity, protect against unwanted energies, and keep your pendulum functioning at its best. This chapter covers my favorite methods for each of these protective measures.

Grounding Exercises to Do Before Using a Pendulum

Grounding is the process of connecting with the earth's energy to stabilize your own energy field. Grounding helps release any scattered or excessive energy, creating a centered and calm state that enhances focus and clarity. Being grounded before using a pendulum allows you to connect with it from a balanced, neutral space.

Favorite Grounding Techniques

Tree Root Visualization

This visualization is a simple yet powerful way to ground your energy. Close your eyes, and imagine roots extending from the soles of your feet, deep into the earth. Visualize these roots moving downward through layers of soil, rock, and bedrock, connecting deeply with the earth's core. As the roots grow, feel a stabilizing energy rising through them into your body, grounding and centering you.

Tip: This method works well with breathwork. With each inhale, imagine drawing in the earth's grounding energy, and with each exhale, release any tension or scattered thoughts.

Earthing or Physical Grounding

Earthing is the practice of making physical contact with the ground to balance your energy field. If possible, take a few minutes to stand barefoot on natural ground, like grass, soil, or sand. This direct connection with the earth's energy helps realign your body's electromagnetic field and can help you feel grounded and present.

Tip: If you're indoors, you can still "earth" by holding a small natural stone, such as hematite or black tourmaline, which have grounding properties.

Centering Breathwork

Breathwork is a quick way to ground your energy if you're short on time. Start by taking slow, deep breaths, focusing on drawing your energy inward. Inhale, count to four, hold for a count of four, then you will exhale for a count of six. As you breathe, imagine your body and mind connecting with a calm, centered space within you.

Tip: Focus on feeling your weight centered in your body, as if you're anchoring yourself to the earth. This technique is portable, making it ideal if you need grounding on the go.

Each of these grounding exercises prepares you to work with your pendulum from a stable, energetically neutral place, ensuring clarity and focus in your work.

Cleansing and Protecting the Pendulum Between Uses

Regularly cleansing your pendulum is essential for maintaining its purity and responsiveness. Every time you use it, the pendulum can absorb energies from both the environment and the people it interacts with, potentially impacting its accuracy and effectiveness. Cleansing helps release any residual energies so the pendulum remains a clear tool for healing.

Favorite Methods for Cleansing the Pendulum

Smudging with Sage or Palo Santo

Smudging with sage or palo santo is one of the most effective and straightforward ways to cleanse a pendulum. Light the sage or palo santo stick, and hold your pendulum in the smoke, allowing it to be enveloped in the cleansing smoke for several seconds. The smoke purifies the energy field of the pendulum, clearing any residual negativity.

Tip: Move the pendulum through the smoke in a circular motion, or simply hold it until you feel a shift in its energy.

Moonlight Cleansing

Placing your pendulum under the moonlight, especially during a full moon, is another gentle way to cleanse and recharge it. Set the pendulum in a place where it will be exposed to the moon's rays overnight, ideally on a natural surface like a windowsill or outdoor ledge. The moon's energy naturally clears away accumulated energies and reinvigorates the pendulum.

Tip: You can combine this with setting an intention, such as "May this pendulum be purified and restored," to enhance the cleansing effect.

Salt Bed Cleansing

Salt has powerful energy-clearing properties. Place a small bed of salt (sea salt or rock salt works best) in a bowl, and gently set your pendulum on top of it. Leave the pendulum in the salt for several hours or overnight to draw out any unwanted energies. Afterward, discard the salt as it has absorbed the pendulum's residual energy.

Tip: Avoid this method for pendulums made from metals or stones sensitive to salt, as it can damage some materials over time.

Sound Cleansing with a Singing Bowl or Chime

Sound frequencies can also clear energies effectively. Use a singing bowl, chime, or even tuning forks to create a vibration near your pendulum. The sound waves dislodge any lingering energies, creating a fresh, energized field. This method is particularly gentle and is safe for all pendulum materials.

Tip: Allow the sound to wash over the pendulum for at least one to two minutes for a thorough cleanse.

Each of these cleansing methods helps maintain the purity of your pendulum, ensuring that each session begins with a clean energetic slate.

Shielding Techniques to Avoid Absorbing Negative Energies

Shielding is an essential practice for protecting yourself and your pendulum from absorbing negative or unwanted energies. When working with a pendulum, you may encounter energies from other people or environments that can interfere with your own energetic field. Shielding techniques create a boundary that keeps your energy safe and prevents disruptions.

Favorite Shielding Techniques

The Protective Light Bubble Visualization Technique

The protective light bubble is a simple but powerful technique to establish an energetic boundary, shielding you from disruptive or negative influences. By visualizing yourself surrounded by a bubble of pure, radiant light, you create a barrier that only allows beneficial energies in while repelling any unwanted or draining energies. This technique can be used daily or before specific spiritual practices, such as pendulum work, meditation, or energy healing.

Here's a step-by-step guide on how to create and enhance a protective light bubble.

Step 1: Begin with Grounding and Centering

Before creating your protective bubble, it helps to ground yourself. Grounding stabilizes your energy and increases your connection with the earth, which serves as a foundation for your protective shield. You might imagine roots extending from your feet into the earth or take a few deep, centering breaths. Feel yourself becoming present, aware, and connected to the earth's supportive energy.

Step 2: Set a Clear Intention

Setting an intention strengthens the effectiveness of the light bubble. Focus on a specific purpose, like, "I create this bubble to protect my energy and allow only positive, high-frequency energies to enter." This intention defines the bubble's function and aligns your mind and spirit with the visualization process.

Step 3: Visualize the Light Emerging

Close your eyes, take a few deep breaths, and imagine a soft, radiant light glowing within your heart or solar plexus (the area just above your navel). This light is pure, healing, and protective. Visualize it expanding slowly from within you, filling your entire body with warmth and peaceful energy.

Step 4: Extend the Light Outward

Once you feel the light filling your entire body, allow it to expand outward, forming a bubble around you. Picture this bubble as a sphere that extends about an arm's length from your body in every direction, surrounding you completely—above, below, in front, behind, and on either side. The light should feel vibrant, comforting, and completely encasing.

Step 5: Define the Bubble's Color and Properties

Each color carries unique energetic properties, and you can choose the color of your bubble based on the type of protection you need. Here are a few suggestions:

- **White Light**: A general protective color, symbolizing purity, clarity, and universal protection.
- **Golden Light**: Stronger, more resilient, and associated with divine protection; excellent for shielding from intense energies.
- **Violet Light**: Highly spiritual, violet offers protection from negative thoughts and psychic interference, while helping you stay aligned with your higher self.

Visualize your chosen color infusing the light around you, creating an aura that feels strong, impenetrable, and reassuring. Imagine it pulsing with gentle, protective energy that responds to any negative influence by strengthening and holding firm.

Step 6: Reinforce with Affirmations or Mantras

To enhance the bubble's power, reinforce it with protective affirmations or mantras. Silently or aloud, say phrases such as:

- "This bubble surrounds me with love, light, and protection."
- "Only positive, light, and high frequency energies may enter this space."
- "I am safe, supported, and protected at all times."

These affirmations help fortify the shield and remind your subconscious mind of the bubble's purpose.

Step 7: Seal the Bubble with Intentional Imagery

To solidify the bubble, visualize its outer layer thickening slightly, creating a boundary that seals in positive energy and deflects anything negative. You might imagine the bubble shimmering or emitting a gentle hum, like a shield that maintains its structure as you move about. Feel free to imagine additional protective properties, such as a soft mirror-like quality that reflects negative energy away or an energetic filter that only allows supportive energies through.

Step 8: Connect with the Bubble's Protection Throughout Your Practice

While working with a pendulum or engaging in any other spiritual practice, maintain an awareness of the bubble surrounding you. If you start to feel overwhelmed or sense unwanted energies, take a moment to strengthen the bubble in your mind by reinforcing its color, brightness, or boundaries. Even a quick mental reminder, such as "I am protected," can instantly reinforce the bubble's protective qualities.

Step 9: Refresh and Release the Bubble as Needed

When you've completed your pendulum work or any energy practice, you can either keep the bubble intact for ongoing protection or release it. To release, simply visualize the bubble gently dissolving, sending any residual energy back into the universe with gratitude. If you choose to keep it, visualize it remaining strong and radiant, providing you with ongoing protection as you go about your day.

Enhancements and Tips for the Light Bubble Technique

1. **Daily Practice**

   Practicing this technique regularly helps you strengthen and stabilize your light bubble quickly. Over time, you may find that simply visualizing the light around you creates an immediate sense of calm and protection.

2. **Use Crystals to Amplify Protection**

   Holding a grounding or protective crystal, like black tourmaline or amethyst, while creating your bubble can reinforce its strength. You can even place a small crystal in your pocket or wear it as jewelry for continuous protection throughout the day.

3. **Incorporate Aromatherapy**

   Essential oils like lavender, sage, or frankincense are known for their protective and grounding qualities. Anoint your pulse points or diffuse these oils to enhance the visualization of your bubble and deepen the sense of safety and peace.

4. **Practice in Nature**

   If possible, try this visualization technique outdoors. Nature's grounding and nurturing energy can help enhance your visualization, making it easier to connect with the sense of protection and peace the bubble provides.

The protective light bubble technique is a versatile and powerful way to maintain a safe energetic space during your pendulum work and beyond. As you make this a regular practice, you'll likely find that your bubble becomes an effortless and effective shield, allowing you to engage fully and confidently in your energy work. This technique can be customized as you grow in your practice, evolving into a deeply personal and reliable method of protection.

Tip: You can customize the color of the bubble to fit your intention: white for general protection, gold for a stronger barrier, or violet for spiritual protection.

Crystal Shielding with Black Tourmaline or Obsidian

Crystal shielding with stones like black tourmaline or obsidian is a powerful technique to protect your energy from negative influences and enhance your energetic resilience during pendulum work or any other spiritual practice. These stones are known for their grounding and protective properties, forming a strong energetic barrier against low-vibration energies, psychic attacks, or emotional disturbances. By using a crystal shield, you can maintain focus and clarity while keeping your energy field clear and secure.

Here's a step-by-step guide on how to use black tourmaline or obsidian for crystal shielding.

Step 1: Cleanse Your Crystal

Before beginning, it's important to cleanse your black tourmaline or obsidian to remove any residual energy. You can cleanse the stone by:

- **Running it under cool water for a few minutes** (make sure the stone is water-safe, as some minerals are sensitive).
- **Smoke from sacred herbs** like palo santo or sage.
- **Leaving it under moonlight** for a few hours, especially on a full moon, to restore its energetic purity.

Cleansing removes any energy the stone has absorbed, ensuring it's clear and ready for your protective work.

Step 2: Hold the Crystal and Set an Intention

Once your crystal is cleansed, hold it in your dominant hand or place it over your heart or solar plexus chakra. You will then close your eyes and take a few deep centering breaths. Set a clear and specific intention for protection, grounding, or energy shielding. For example, you might say:

- "I charge this crystal to shield me from all negative or disruptive energies."

- "May this black tourmaline/obsidian create a strong, protective barrier around me, allowing only positive, supportive energies to enter my space."

This intention will align the crystal's energy with your purpose, activating its protective properties and helping it sync with your own energy.

Step 3: Visualize a Protective Energetic Field

With your eyes closed and the crystal in hand, visualize a radiant, protective field beginning to form around you. Imagine the energy of the black tourmaline or obsidian amplifying and expanding, encasing you in a shield. This shield might look like a dense, black aura that repels any unwanted influences or as a translucent, glowing field with grounding roots that connect you to the earth.

Feel the grounding effect of the crystal pulling away any negativity, distractions, or imbalances and keeping you centered. As the visualization strengthens, sense the crystal creating a stable, secure boundary that blocks out any energies not aligned with your highest good.

Step 4: Place the Crystal Around You (Optional)

For added support, you can place the crystal around you in specific ways:

- **Wear it as jewelry**: Many people wear black tourmaline or obsidian as a necklace, bracelet, or ring, keeping it close to their body. This way, the stone stays in contact with your energy field throughout the day, maintaining continuous protection.

- **Keep it in your pocket**: Holding the crystal in your pocket can create a portable shield that strengthens whenever you're holding or touching it.
- **Create a grid**: For stationary energy work, like pendulum readings, place four pieces of black tourmaline or obsidian at the four corners of your workspace, forming a grid that surrounds and protects you.

Step 5: Reinforce the Shield with Affirmations

Using affirmations while holding or wearing the crystal can enhance its protective effects. Some affirmations you might try include:

- "This crystal surrounds me with a shield of grounding and protection."
- "I am safe and I am grounded in my protective field."
- "Negative energy cannot penetrate this boundary; only positive and supportive energy flows through."

Repeat these affirmations a few times, feeling the crystal's energy amplify and reinforce the shield.

Step 6: Trust the Crystal's Protection and Remain Grounded

After completing your visualization and affirmations, trust that the crystal is actively working to protect you. Throughout your practice, periodically touch or focus on the stone to ground yourself if you feel distracted or sense any energetic interference. Black tourmaline and obsidian are strong grounding stones, so simply connecting with them for a moment can restore balance and stability in your field.

Step 7: Cleanse the Crystal After Each Use

Once you've finished using the crystal for protection, be sure to cleanse it again to release any negative energy it may have absorbed. Regular cleansing maintains the stone's potency and helps it continue working at its full protective capacity for each session.

Enhancements and Variations of the Crystal Shielding Technique

Here are additional ways to strengthen and personalize your crystal shielding technique:

1. **Combine with Other Stones**
   Pairing black tourmaline or obsidian with other protective or grounding stones, such as amethyst or hematite, can create an even stronger shield. For example, amethyst adds a spiritual protection layer, while hematite enhances grounding and stability.

2. **Use Essential Oils**

    Applying grounding essential oils, like cedarwood or frankincense, to your pulse points before holding the crystal can deepen your grounding and protection. These oils are known for their calming and centering effects, helping you stay in a clear, balanced state.

3. **Practice in Nature**

    If possible, practice this shielding technique outdoors or in a natural setting, as nature's grounding energy can amplify the stone's protective qualities. Standing barefoot on grass or soil while holding black tourmaline or obsidian can help you connect more deeply with its grounding power.

4. **Place the Crystal Under Your Pillow for Nighttime Protection**

    If you want to extend your protection during sleep, try placing black tourmaline or obsidian under your pillow or by your bedside. This practice is believed to shield you from disruptive energies, promote restful sleep, and keep your energy balanced even at night.

5. **Carry a Small Piece in Your Bag or Car**

    Keeping a piece of black tourmaline or obsidian in your bag, car, or workspace can act as an ongoing shield that protects your energy wherever you go. This portable shield is especially useful if you're moving through environments with unpredictable energies.

Crystal shielding with black tourmaline or obsidian is an effective and adaptable practice that supports you in maintaining a safe, grounded, and protected energetic field. This technique can become a go-to method for feeling empowered and secure, regardless of the spiritual work you're engaging in. With regular use, you'll likely find that these stones enhance your confidence, allowing you to connect deeply with your pendulum and other energy practices while remaining safe and grounded.

Invocation of Protective Intentions or Affirmations

Invoking protective intentions or affirmations is a powerful technique for setting up a mental and energetic shield around yourself before working with a pendulum or engaging in any type of spiritual or energy work. By consciously aligning your intentions, you create a vibration that naturally repels unwanted energies and attracts supportive forces. Affirmations and intentions are not only mental exercises but also vibrational cues that shape the energy around you, setting a protective foundation for your practice.

Here's a step-by-step guide on invoking protective intentions or affirmations, along with ways to enhance this technique for deeper effectiveness.

Step 1: Create a Centered, Focused Space

Begin by finding a calm, quiet space where you can focus without interruptions. You might dim the lights, light a candle, or play soft music to create an atmosphere that supports a peaceful state of mind. This calm environment helps you concentrate fully on your intentions and establish a solid mental foundation.

Step 2: Take a Few Grounding Breaths

Before calling forth your affirmations, take a few deep breaths to center yourself. Focus on the rise and fall of your breath, allowing any stress or tension to dissipate. With each exhale, release any negativity or anxiety. Imagine grounding your energy to the earth, becoming rooted and present. This grounding process aligns you with a balanced, receptive state and prepares you to set clear and powerful intentions.

Step 3: Speak or Think Your Protective Intentions

Now, begin to silently or verbally state your protective intentions. These intentions should be clear, specific, and affirmative, helping you set the purpose and boundaries for your work. Here are some examples of effective protective intentions:

- "I call forth a shield of light to surround me and to protect me during this session."

- "Only light beings and high-vibrational energies are welcome in my space."
- "I am protected and supported by universal light and love."
- "My energy is grounded, safe, and is not affected by unwanted influences or energies."

Feel free to personalize these intentions to suit your specific needs. Speak them with conviction and clarity, imagining each word reinforcing a strong energetic boundary around you.

Step 4: Reinforce the Intention with Visualization

To deepen the protection, visualize your words taking shape as a glowing sphere of energy surrounding you. As you say each phrase, imagine the energy of the intention expanding, brightening, and strengthening. You might picture each affirmation as a burst of light, forming layers of energy around you until you feel securely enveloped in a safe, radiant shield.

Step 5: Use Repetition to Build Strength

Repetition is a powerful way to anchor your affirmations. You might repeat your protective intentions three, five, or even ten times, with each repetition deepening your focus and connection to the energy. Each time, feel the words resonating more profoundly, creating a stable, protective vibration around you.

Step 6: Feel the Protection Surrounding You

After you've repeated your intentions, pause for a moment and feel the protective energy around you. Trust that your words have formed a real and active shield. Notice any sensations of warmth, peace, or strength; this is the energy of your intention at work, creating a barrier that supports your highest good.

Step 7: Anchor the Protection with a Closing Affirmation

To seal the invocation, close with a final affirmation, such as:

- "I am fully protected and guided."
- "My energy is safe, grounded, and secure."
- "This protection will hold for the duration of my work and beyond."

These closing words act as an energetic seal, anchoring the protective boundary for as long as you need it.

Enhanced Methods for Protective Intentions and Affirmations

Here are a few techniques to further amplify your protective invocation:

1. **Incorporate Physical Touch**

   Adding a physical component to your invocation,

like placing a hand over your heart or solar plexus, can enhance the connection. This touch grounds the intention physically, while also reinforcing the affirmation with a sense of presence and embodiment.

2. **Write Down Your Intentions**
    Writing your protective intentions on paper can create a lasting energetic imprint. You can keep the paper nearby as you work, fold it under a crystal, or burn it afterward (safely) to send the intention into the universe. This method allows you to focus on the words even more deeply.

3. **Use Crystals as Amplifiers**
    Holding or placing protective stones, such as black tourmaline, amethyst, or selenite, during your invocation strengthens the intention. Crystals naturally vibrate at high frequencies, enhancing the energy of your affirmations and creating an additional layer of protection.

4. **Incorporate Aromatherapy**
    Essential oils like frankincense, lavender, or sage can further heighten the protective energy. Place a drop on your wrists or diffuse the oil in your space while you recite your intentions. These oils are known for their grounding and protective qualities, adding an extra sensory layer to the practice.

5. **Chanting or Singing Your Intentions**
    If you feel comfortable, try chanting or singing your

affirmations. The vibration of sound amplifies the energetic resonance of your words, making the intention more potent and dynamic. Each tone creates a unique frequency that can act as a barrier against unwanted energies.

6. **Use Sacred Symbols or Gestures**
    Adding symbols like a cross, an ankh, or another spiritual emblem you connect with can amplify the affirmation. Draw or visualize this symbol around you while invoking your intentions, adding a layer of spiritual or cultural significance to the protection.

7. Invoking protective intentions or affirmations is a versatile technique that you can personalize and adapt to suit any environment or need. As you practice, you may find that these words and visualizations come more naturally and instantly activate a sense of security and grounding. This practice builds a strong foundation for all your pendulum and energy work, empowering you to stay safe, centered, and in control of your own energy field.

Tip: Repeating this intention throughout your pendulum work can help reinforce your protective shield, especially during long sessions.

The Mirroring Shield Technique

The mirroring shield technique is a powerful and protective visualization exercise that creates an energetic boundary around you by reflecting any negative or disruptive energies back to their origin. This shield doesn't absorb or transmute unwanted energy; instead, it deflects it away from your field, preserving your personal energy and preventing outside influences from interfering with your work. This technique is especially helpful when working in intense environments or when you anticipate encountering strong emotional or energetic currents.

Here's a step-by-step guide to practicing the mirroring shield technique:

Step 1: Find a Centered, Quiet Space

Begin by grounding yourself in a comfortable and quiet environment. You may wish to perform a quick grounding exercise, like the Tree Root Visualization or centering breathwork, to feel calm and present. Grounding before shielding creates a stable energetic foundation and helps strengthen the shield.

Step 2: Set Your Intention

Setting a clear intention is key to activating the shield. You can silently or verbally affirm something like:

"I create a protective mirror shield around myself, reflecting only positive energy inward and redirecting all negative or disruptive energy away from my field."

This intention sets the purpose of the shield and strengthens your focus on what you're about to create.

Step 3: Visualize the Shield's Formation

With your eyes closed, imagine a sphere of light beginning to form around you, extending about an arm's length in all directions. This sphere will soon become your mirroring shield. Picture it expanding smoothly around you, completely surrounding your body in a seamless, protective layer.

Step 4: Transform the Shield into a Reflective Surface

Now, visualize this sphere of light turning into a mirrored surface, like the exterior of a polished, reflective bubble. Picture it shimmering, almost like liquid metal, or as a smooth, glassy surface with a strong reflection. This mirrored surface should be facing outward, so any energy directed toward you will be reflected away. The strength and clarity of your visualization reinforce the shield's potency.

Step 5: Strengthen the Shield with Affirmations

Once you've visualized the mirrored sphere, reinforce it with protective affirmations. Repeat phrases like:

- "This shield reflects all negative energy back to its source."
- "Only positive and uplifting energy can pass through this shield."
- "I am protected, grounded, and unaffected by unwanted influences."

These affirmations help solidify your intention and strengthen the shield.

Step 6: Program the Shield's Function

You can program the shield with specific functions if you're seeking a more tailored level of protection. For example, you might instruct the shield to allow loving, supportive energies in while keeping out disruptive or draining ones. To do this, simply visualize the shield filtering energies according to your preference, like a one-way mirror that selectively admits only beneficial energies.

Step 7: Maintain Your Shield During Pendulum Work

While working with your pendulum, maintain an awareness of your shield. You may occasionally re-visualize the mirror's surface or silently reaffirm your intention to keep the shield active. This awareness can be subtle and doesn't need to interrupt your focus but rather reinforces your protection as you interact with your pendulum's energy.

Step 8: Dissolve the Shield (After the Session)

When you've finished your pendulum work or when you feel you no longer need the shield, take a moment to dissolve it. Visualize the mirrored surface gently fading or returning to light before disappearing completely. Thank the shield for its protection, and take a few deep breaths to return to a neutral state.

Tip: Use this technique when working in emotionally charged environments or with others who may have intense energies, as it helps keep your space protected.

Herbal and Essential Oil Shielding Technique

Using herbs and essential oils for energetic shielding is a natural and aromatic way to enhance your spiritual practice and protect yourself from unwanted energies. Many herbs and oils possess protective, purifying, and grounding properties that can create a powerful shield around you. By incorporating herbal and essential oil shielding into your practice, you can elevate your energy, maintain clarity, and protect your aura in a gentle yet effective manner.

Here's a step-by-step guide on how to use herbs and essential oils for shielding.

Step 1: Choose Your Herbs and Essential Oils

Select herbs and essential oils that are known for their protective and grounding qualities. Here are a few popular options:

- **Sage**: Purifying and clearing, sage helps remove negative energy and creates a fresh, protected space.
- **Frankincense**: Known for its spiritual properties, frankincense promotes a sense of calm, grounding, and energetic protection.
- **Cedarwood**: A grounding and protective oil, cedarwood enhances stability and creates a shield around your aura.
- **Lavender**: Soothing and calming, lavender provides a gentle shield against stress and negativity.
- **Rosemary**: Cleansing and energizing, rosemary protects against unwanted influences and strengthens your natural defenses.
- **Mugwort**: Often used in spiritual practices, mugwort promotes psychic protection and mental clarity.
- **Black Pepper**: This oil has a warming, protective effect, creating a strong barrier against negativity.

Choose one or a blend of these oils or herbs based on what resonates with you and the kind of protection you feel you need.

Step 2: Create Your Protective Blend

If using essential oils, you can create a blend by combining a few drops of your chosen oils in a small glass bottle with a carrier oil, like jojoba, coconut, or sweet almond oil. Here's a simple recipe to start:

Protective Shielding Oil Blend:

- 5 drops of frankincense essential oil
- 4 drops of cedarwood essential oil
- 3 drops of rosemary essential oil
- 3 drops of lavender essential oil
- 2 drops of sage essential oil

Mix the oils in a 10 ml bottle with a carrier oil. Shake gently to combine.

For a herbal blend, consider creating a small sachet or bundle with dried versions of these herbs. You can carry this sachet in your pocket or bag, place it near your workspace, or even hold it during meditation.

Step 3: Anoint Yourself or Your Space

If using an essential oil blend, apply a small amount to pulse points like your wrists, behind your ears, or on your temples. You can also place a bit over your heart, solar plexus, or on the soles of your feet to ground yourself further. As you apply, visualize the oil creating a protective, energetic layer around your body. Imagine it forming a subtle, glowing shield that fortifies your energy and repels unwanted influences.

For a herbal blend, gently crush or rub the herbs in your hands to release their fragrance, then breathe in deeply. You can also wave the sachet around your body or space, visualizing the herbal energy surrounding you with protection.

Step 4: Create a Protective Mist (Optional)

If you prefer a spray, make a protective mist by mixing your essential oils with distilled water and a pinch of sea salt in a small spray bottle. Shake well before each use. Mist yourself, your workspace, or any area you want to protect. This mist can be used before pendulum work or meditation, creating an aromatic shield that enhances focus and protection.

Protective Mist Recipe:

- 10 drops of lavender essential oil
- 8 drops of rosemary essential oil
- 5 drops of frankincense essential oil
- 1 tablespoon of witch hazel (as an emulsifier)
- Fill the rest of the bottle with distilled water

Shake well and spray around yourself or your environment as needed.

Step 5: Visualize the Protective Shield

After anointing yourself or misting, close your eyes and focus on the aroma. Visualize the scent expanding outward, forming a protective bubble around you. Imagine this aromatic shield as a filter, allowing only positive, high-vibration energy to pass through while deflecting any negative or disruptive energy.

If using a sachet, hold it in your hands, close your eyes, and visualize its energy blending with yours, forming a shield around your aura.

Step 6: Set an Intention for Protection

While breathing in the fragrance of your chosen herbs or oils, set an intention for protection. You might say something like:

- "I am surrounded by a protective shield. It repels all negative energy."
- "These herbs shield me from harm and allow only positive high vibrational energy to enter my space."
- "I am safe, grounded, and supported by the energies of the earth."

Repeating this intention helps to anchor the shielding effect of the herbs or oils and amplifies the protection.

Step 7: Reinforce Throughout the Day (Optional)

If needed, reapply or remist your blend throughout the day. Each application can remind you of your shield and keep your energy grounded and protected.

If you're carrying a sachet, you can hold it in your hands periodically or keep it near you when you feel you need extra protection. The subtle presence of the herbs creates a continuous barrier that refreshes your energy and acts as a gentle reminder of your protected state.

Enhancements and Variations for Herbal and Essential Oil Shielding

1. **Add Crystals to Your Herbal Sachet**
   Small protective crystals like black tourmaline, amethyst, or smoky quartz can enhance the herbal blend. These stones work well with herbs, amplifying the protective energy.

2. **Create a Sacred Ritual**
   For a deeper connection, consider incorporating this technique into a small ritual. Light a candle, set your oils or herbs around it, and spend a few moments focusing on your intention. The candlelight can add an additional layer of protective energy.

3. **Use Herbal Smoke**

   If you're comfortable with smoke cleansing, burn dried sage, rosemary, or mugwort as a smoke shield around yourself. Wave the smoke gently around your body, visualizing it sealing you in a bubble of protection.

4. **Essential Oil Bath**

   Add a few drops of your protective oils to a warm bath along with Epsom salt. This bath can help you release any accumulated negativity and create a shield around you that lasts even after you've finished the bath.

5. **Create an Herb and Oil Protection Jar**

   Fill a small jar with protective herbs and oils. Keep this jar near your workspace, meditation space, or bedside as an ongoing source of protection.

By using herbal and essential oil shielding, you're working with nature's gifts to create a grounded, secure, and protective atmosphere. This technique not only surrounds you with powerful protection but also connects you with the ancient tradition of plant-based energy work. As you build a routine with these herbs and oils, they'll become powerful allies, helping you maintain clarity, balance, and peace in your energetic field.

Tip: You can anoint your hands with a few drops of protective essential oil (like rosemary or frankincense) before starting your pendulum session to strengthen your energetic shield.

Working with pendulums can bring insightful guidance and profound healing experiences, but maintaining energetic safety is key to ensuring these benefits. Protective measures—grounding, cleansing, and shielding—not only keep your energy field balanced but also enhance the clarity and reliability of your pendulum work. Incorporating these practices will help you feel empowered, safe, and ready to engage with the pendulum's energy in the most positive and transformative way. Over time, you'll find that these protective habits deepen your connection with your pendulum and foster a stable, clear environment for all your healing and divination practices.

Chapter 6: Advanced Healing Practices

Techniques for Using Pendulums in Space Clearing and Energy Alignment

Pendulums are not only useful for personal healing and guidance but can also be powerful tools for space clearing and energy alignment. Every space has its own energy field, influenced by the emotions, intentions, and activities that occur within it. Over time, energy can stagnate, become blocked, or accumulate negative vibrations, affecting the well-being of those who occupy it. Using a pendulum to clear and realign energy in a space can bring harmony, peace, and renewed vitality.

Here, we'll explore several techniques for using pendulums to cleanse, align, and uplift the energy of your surroundings.

Preparing for Space Clearing and Alignment

Before you begin, set an intention for the clearing and alignment process. Decide what kind of energy you want to cultivate in the space (such as peace, creativity, or grounding) and visualize how you want it to feel. This will help your pendulum work more effectively by aligning it with your clear and focused intentions.

Recommended Steps to Prepare:

1. **Select the Right Pendulum**

   For space clearing and energy alignment, a pendulum with protective or cleansing properties is ideal. Crystals like amethyst, clear quartz, black tourmaline, and selenite are excellent choices, as they are known for their ability to transmute, purify, and balance energy.

2. **Cleanse Your Pendulum**

   To ensure that your pendulum is energetically neutral, cleanse it before starting. You can hold it under running water (if the material allows), leave it in sunlight or moonlight, or smudge it with sage or palo santo smoke. This process removes any lingering energies and prepares the pendulum for effective work.

3. **Ground and Center Yourself**

   Since space clearing can involve shifting a lot of energy, it's important to ground yourself. Take a few deep breaths, visualize roots extending from your feet into the earth, and connect with a calm, centered feeling. Grounding helps you stay balanced and protected while working with your pendulum.

Technique 1: Space Clearing with the Pendulum

Pendulums can effectively clear stagnant or negative energy from rooms, homes, and other spaces. Here's how to use your pendulum for space clearing:

- **Determine the Energy Level of the Space**
  Begin by standing in the center of the room or space you want to clear. Hold your pendulum steady and ask it to show you the current energy state of the space. You might say, "Show me the energy level in this space." Observe the pendulum's movements:

  - **Clockwise Circles** often indicate positive or neutral energy.
  - **Counterclockwise Circles** can suggest stagnant or negative energy.
  - **Swinging Side to Side or Back and Forth** could mean mixed or unbalanced energy.

2. **Identify Specific Areas Needing Clearing**
   Walk slowly around the space with your pendulum. Hold it over different areas, corners, furniture, and entry points, allowing it to detect energetic imbalances. When the pendulum exhibits counterclockwise or erratic movement, note these areas as spots where energy clearing is needed.

3. **Clear the Energy**

To clear the energy in problem areas, hold the pendulum over them and request that any negative, stagnant, or unwanted energy be released. Imagine a cleansing light surrounding the pendulum, radiating out to purify the space. You can also ask the pendulum directly to remove any negative or disruptive energies.

Allow the pendulum to move freely; it may begin swinging in counterclockwise circles as it works to clear the energy. Once the space feels lighter, the pendulum may slow down or shift to a clockwise motion, indicating the clearing is complete.

4. **Seal the Space with Positive Energy**

After clearing, go back to the center of the room and ask the pendulum to infuse the space with positive, uplifting energy. Visualize the energy you desire—peace, joy, or clarity—filling the room. Allow the pendulum to rotate clockwise, creating a protective, harmonious energy field.

5. **Repeat as Needed**

For large or heavily used spaces, consider repeating this process in multiple areas of the room or conducting regular clearings to maintain balanced energy.

Technique 2: Energy Alignment for Specific Purposes

Once the space is cleared, you can use your pendulum to align the energy in a way that supports specific intentions, like improving focus in a workspace, promoting relaxation in a bedroom, or enhancing creativity in an art studio.

1. **Set a Clear Intention**

    Start by identifying what type of energy you want to bring into the space. For example, if you're working in an office, you may want to align the energy for focus and productivity. In a meditation room, you might aim for a calm and grounding environment.

2. **Ask the Pendulum to Align the Energy**

    Hold your pendulum in the center of the space and state your intention aloud or in your mind. For example, "I ask that the energy in this space be aligned for peace and calm." As you make this request, visualize the pendulum harmonizing the energy to match your desired outcome.

3. **Observe the Pendulum's Movements**

    Watch the pendulum's motion as it works to align the energy. A clockwise circle often indicates that energy is becoming balanced, while shifts in direction can suggest that additional work is needed. Trust the pendulum to move in a way that directs energy alignment as needed.

4. **Anchor the Energy**

    Once the pendulum's movements become steady
    and the space feels aligned with your intention, vi-
    sualize the energy solidifying within the room. You
    might imagine an invisible layer of this desired en-
    ergy settling throughout the space, enhancing its
    atmosphere and supporting its purpose.

5. **Reaffirm with Positive Intentions**

    To anchor this alignment, repeat positive affirma-
    tions for the space. Examples might include:

- "This room is filled with creative inspiration."
- "This space supports calm, peace, and rejuvenation."
- "Productive, focused energy fills this workspace."

Repeating affirmations aligns the energy with a positive
intention, which the pendulum helps reinforce.

Technique 3: Clearing Energy Pathways in Your Home or Workspace

Beyond individual rooms, you can use a pendulum to clear
and align the entire energy pathway within your home or
workspace. This technique is particularly helpful if your
environment feels tense, chaotic, or draining.

1. **Walk Along Main Pathways**

   Begin by walking along the main paths in your space, such as the entryway, hallway, and around primary gathering areas (like a living room or kitchen). Hold your pendulum in each space, allowing it to pick up on any areas of blockages or stagnant energy.

2. **Clear Blockages in Pathways**

   When the pendulum indicates a blockage, use the clearing process described earlier, allowing it to move counterclockwise to release any heavy or stagnant energy. Imagine these pathways becoming clear, allowing energy to flow freely.

3. **Align Pathways with Positive Flow**

   After clearing, ask the pendulum to align the pathways with a positive flow of energy. Picture the energy moving smoothly and unobstructed throughout the entire space. You might visualize light streaming through every pathway, illuminating it and creating a clear, energetic channel.

4. **Conduct a Final Check at Key Entry Points**

   Stand at key entry points, like doorways or windows, and hold your pendulum there to check for any lingering energy disturbances. These areas are where external energies can enter, so aligning them with positive, protective energy helps prevent outside negativity from affecting your space.

Personal Experience: Space Clearing in My Home

In my own practice, I once used these techniques in my meditation space, which had started feeling cluttered and heavy despite regular cleaning. My pendulum picked up on stagnant energy in one corner where I stored books and supplies. I used the clearing technique, visualizing light washing over the corner and inviting fresh energy to circulate. Afterward, the space felt noticeably lighter, and my meditations became clearer and more focused.

Another time, I used the pendulum to clear and align my workspace. By setting intentions for focus and productivity, I transformed a previously chaotic area into a calm, efficient zone. The process was empowering, reminding me of the influence we have over our environments through intention and energy work.

Using a pendulum to clear and align spaces is a valuable skill that enhances the harmony and energy of any environment. As you work with these techniques, you'll find that your surroundings support your personal growth, well-being, and peace. This practice can be an empowering addition to your pendulum work, allowing you to create spaces that feel safe, vibrant, and aligned with your highest intentions.

Chapter 7: Developing Your Intuition

Strengthening Intuitive Skills with Pendulum Work

Pendulums are not only practical tools for healing and energy work but also powerful instruments for enhancing intuitive skills. By working with a pendulum, you can develop a deeper connection with your inner guidance system, build trust in your instincts, and amplify your natural intuition. This practice can help you become more attuned to subtle energies, allowing you to make more intuitive decisions in your healing practice and everyday life.

In this section, we will explore various techniques and exercises for strengthening your intuitive skills through pendulum work.

Cultivating Awareness: The Foundation of Intuition

The first step in developing intuition is cultivating awareness of the subtle messages and sensations within your own body and mind. Pendulum work enhances this awareness, as it requires you to focus, attune to energy, and observe nuances in movement. Start by creating a regular practice of checking in with your body, emotions, and surroundings when you use your pendulum.

Exercise: Setting an Intention for Intuitive Awareness

1. **Find a Quiet Space:** Begin by sitting in a calm, quiet area where you won't be disturbed. Hold your pendulum in your hand and take a few deep breaths to center yourself.

2. **Set an Intention:** State a clear intention for developing your intuition. You might say, "I intend to strengthen my intuition and become attuned to my inner guidance."

3. **Focus on Sensations:** Gently observe how your body feels as you hold your pendulum. Notice any tingling in your hands, warmth in your chest, or a sense of calmness in your mind. These physical responses are often the body's way of communicating intuitive insights.

4. **Ask for Guidance:** With your pendulum, ask, "What do I need to be aware of to strengthen my intuition?" Observe how the pendulum moves, and trust that its direction holds insight into what you need.

Practicing this exercise regularly can help you become more in tune with subtle shifts in energy and increase your awareness, laying a strong foundation for intuition.

Techniques for Tuning into Intuition Using the Pendulum

Working with a pendulum is a direct way to build a connection with your inner wisdom. By practicing specific techniques, you can learn to differentiate between logical thinking and intuitive guidance, a key aspect of developing strong intuitive skills.

Technique 1: Yes/No Responses to Build Trust in Inner Guidance

The yes/no technique is a fundamental pendulum practice and can be a valuable tool for building trust in your intuition. Asking simple yes/no questions allows you to practice reading the pendulum's responses and tune into your inner "gut" feelings.

1. **Establish Your Yes/No Baseline:**
    Hold your pendulum in a relaxed, steady manner. Ask a question with a known answer, like "Is my name [your name]?" to determine how your pendulum indicates "yes." Do the same with a question that you know will yield a "no" response, such as "Am I 10 feet tall?" Take note of the pendulum's specific movement for "yes" and "no," as these motions will become your baseline.

2.   **Practice with Everyday Questions:**
     To build confidence, ask simple yes/no questions throughout the day. For example, "Is it in my best interest to attend this meeting?" or "Should I call this person back now?" As you become familiar with the pendulum's responses, notice any intuitive sensations, such as a sense of excitement, relief, or resistance.

3.   **Tune into Inner Sensations Alongside Pendulum Movements:**
     When your pendulum gives a response, observe any bodily sensations. You may feel a calm, grounded sense with a "yes" or a slight discomfort with a "no." By paying attention to these sensations, you'll begin to identify your intuition's unique signals, separate from thoughts or emotions.

Technique 2: Asking Open-Ended Questions for Intuitive Insights

The pendulum can be used for more than yes/no questions; it can also guide you with open-ended questions, where the response is less about direction and more about insight. This technique enhances intuition by allowing you to connect with your deeper wisdom and interpret the pendulum's movements intuitively.

1. **Choose a Question Related to Personal Growth:**
    Ask a question like, "What do I need to know to develop my intuitive skills?" or "What aspect of my intuition should I focus on today?" Hold your pendulum over a neutral space, such as your palm, and observe how it moves.

2. **Interpret the Movement Beyond Yes/No:**
    For open-ended questions, your pendulum may make a variety of movements, such as spinning in a circle, making small waves, or moving side-to-side. Each movement can be interpreted based on your intuitive sense, or you can use these responses to guide your thoughts and reflections. A circle may indicate cycles or repetition, while a side-to-side motion could suggest a need for balance.

3. **Journal Your Insights:**
    After asking open-ended questions, write down your impressions, observations, and any intuitive insights you receive. Over time, you'll notice patterns and deepen your understanding of the pendulum's language and how it resonates with your intuition.

Technique 3: Developing "Yes, And" Responses for Deeper Intuitive Understanding

"Yes, and" responses involve using the pendulum to confirm an answer, then layering it with a follow-up question.

This technique helps you move beyond surface-level responses, developing your ability to sense the energy behind each answer.

1. **Ask a Simple Question and Observe the Response:**

   Begin by asking a yes/no question, such as, "Is this the right time to start a new project?" Wait for your pendulum's response.

2. **Follow with a "Yes, And" Question:**

   After receiving your answer, build on it by asking a follow-up question. For example, if the answer is "yes," you might ask, "Yes, and is there anything I need to know to proceed successfully?" This practice allows you to go deeper and strengthen your ability to sense layered guidance.

3. **Listen to Both Movement and Inner Impressions:**

   As you ask each follow-up, tune into the pendulum's movement and your inner reactions. A small wave or change in direction may suggest additional considerations, while your own sensations can hint at your intuition's subtle cues. This practice refines your ability to hear layered, multi-dimensional answers.

Personal Reflection: Building Trust in Intuition Through Pendulum Work

When I first started using a pendulum to strengthen my intuition, I realized that trusting my responses was the biggest challenge. At times, I questioned whether my hand was moving the pendulum or if I was misinterpreting its movements. However, as I continued to practice, I learned to recognize the calm feeling that accompanied genuine intuitive responses.

In one instance, I used the pendulum to help make a decision about whether to pursue a new opportunity. The pendulum gave a clear "yes" response, and with it, I felt a subtle, uplifting sensation in my chest. Trusting both the pendulum's answer and my bodily intuition, I followed through and found that the opportunity aligned perfectly with my path.

Exercises for Deepening Your Connection with Intuition

Here are some exercises to try regularly as part of your pendulum practice. By incorporating these into your daily or weekly routine, you'll grow more attuned to your inner guidance.

1. **Daily Intuition Check-In**
   Start each day by holding your pendulum and asking, "What should I be aware of today?" Let the pendulum swing freely, and take note of its movement. Reflect on this response and keep it in mind throughout your day. This exercise helps you be-

come more in tune with your intuition's subtle guidance.

2. **Intuitive Symbols Practice**
    Draw three symbols on a piece of paper: one representing "yes," one for "no," and one for "maybe." Hold your pendulum over each symbol and ask it to show which represents its "yes" response, "no," and "maybe" answers. This visual exercise can enhance your symbolic interpretation skills, allowing you to incorporate symbols into your pendulum work.

3. **Grounding and Centering Exercise for Intuitive Clarity**
    Before each pendulum session, spend a few minutes grounding yourself. Close your eyes, take deep cleansing breaths, and imagine roots growing from your feet extending deep into the earth. This grounding prepares you to connect with your intuition without interference from stress or distractions, enhancing the clarity of your pendulum work.

Honing Your Intuitive Pendulum Practice

As you practice these techniques, remember that intuition is like a muscle that strengthens with use. Each pendulum session builds trust, sensitivity, and confidence in your intuitive abilities.

The journey to strengthening intuition with pendulum work is deeply personal, and each session offers insights into your own unique way of receiving guidance. Over time, you'll notice how these intuitive insights enhance your daily life, offering clarity, reassurance, and alignment in both your healing practice and everyday choices.

Exercises to Enhance Energy Sensitivities

Strengthening your energy sensitivity is essential for effective pendulum work and intuitive practice. By becoming more aware of subtle energy shifts within yourself and the environment, you can tune into your pendulum's responses with greater clarity and depth. This sensitivity helps you sense blockages, pick up on others' energy fields, and identify underlying emotional or energetic patterns. In this section, we'll explore practical exercises that can build your energy sensitivity, preparing you for more advanced pendulum healing and intuitive work.

Exercise 1: Energy Sensitivity Warm-Up

This simple warm-up exercise helps you recognize and feel your own energy, which is crucial for developing sensitivity to external energy as well.

1. **Rub Your Hands Together**
    Start by rubbing your palms together for about 10–15 seconds. This action creates warmth and brings attention to the energy in your hands, making it easier to sense.

2. **Slowly Separate Your Hands**

   After rubbing your hands, bring them about an inch apart and start slowly moving them closer and farther apart, almost like compressing and expanding an invisible ball. Focus on any sensations between your palms—heat, tingling, or a magnetic-like push or pull.

3. **Experiment with Distance**

   As you continue, move your hands farther apart and closer again, noticing any changes in sensation. If you sense a subtle energetic "bubble" between your hands, you're tuning into your personal energy field.

4. **Take Mental Notes**

   Reflect on what you feel. This exercise can be done daily to increase your sensitivity to energy; over time, you may notice your ability to sense energy extending beyond your own hands, such as around objects or other people.

Exercise 2: Sensing the Energy of Objects

Every object has its own energetic frequency, which can be felt with practice. Tuning into these subtle vibrations can help you understand how different materials feel energetically, which is beneficial when selecting a pendulum or choosing healing objects.

1. **Select a Few Objects**

   Gather items with distinct qualities—something organic like a rock or a leaf, a crystal, a piece of metal, and a glass of water. These diverse materials will each have unique energy vibrations.

2. **Center Yourself**
   Sit quietly, take a few deep breaths, and release any tension. Hold one object in your hand, close your eyes, and focus solely on the sensations it brings. Notice any warmth, coolness, tingling, or shifts in your emotions.

3. **Move the Object Around Your Body**
   Slowly move the object around your body (for example, near your chest, stomach, or head) and observe how its energy feels in each area. Some objects may feel soothing or grounding, while others might feel sharp or energizing.

4. **Record Your Observations**
   Write down your impressions of each object and note any differences. Practicing with different materials strengthens your sensitivity to their unique energies, which can later aid in understanding how different pendulums affect you.

Exercise 3: Energy Scanning

Energy scanning involves sensing subtle energy fields in people, objects, or spaces. This skill can help you become more aware of energy imbalances and blockages, which is invaluable in pendulum healing work.

1. **Begin with Self-Scanning**

   Sit comfortably, close your eyes, and take a few deep breaths to center yourself. Slowly move your hands about an inch away from your body, starting at the top of your head and gradually working down toward your feet.

2. **Notice Changes in Sensation**

   As you move your hands down your body, pay attention to any areas that feel "different." You might feel warmth, tingling, coolness, or even a sense of heaviness. These sensations could signal energetic shifts or areas that need attention.

3. **Try Scanning Another Person or Object**

   Once you're comfortable with self-scanning, try practicing on another person (with permission) or an object, like a plant. Move your hands slowly around the person or object, noticing any changes in sensation. Over time, this can help you become attuned to subtle energy signatures in different things and people.

4. **Jot Down Observations**

   Reflect on any shifts you felt and whether certain areas felt different from others. Energy scanning takes practice, so repeat this exercise frequently to build your sensitivity.

Exercise 4: Visualizing Energy Flows

Visualizing energy flows helps strengthen your awareness
of how energy moves through your body and surroundings.
By practicing energy visualization, you'll become more
sensitive to subtle shifts that might indicate an energy
blockage or imbalance.

1. **Begin with a Grounding Breath**
    Sit quietly, close your eyes, and take deep breaths.
    Visualize roots growing out the bottom of your fee
    and extending deep into the earth. As you exhale,
    feel any tension draining into the ground.

2. **Visualize Energy Moving Through Your Body**
    Imagine a warm, golden light entering the top of
    your head, flowing down through your spine, and
    branching out into each limb. Picture this energy
    filling every part of your body, feeling warmth or
    tingling as it moves.

3. **Focus on Areas of Sensitivity**
    If there are areas where the energy flow feels
    blocked, heavy, or different, pause and observe any

sensations. This can help you become more aware of subtle imbalances in your energy field.

4. **Use This Awareness in Pendulum Work**
   Practicing visualization exercises like this will make it easier to notice energy flows when you work with a pendulum, as your body becomes more attuned to subtle energetic shifts.

Exercise 5: Energy Resonance with Nature

Nature has a grounding, balancing energy that can help you tune into subtle energies. Practicing energy sensitivity outdoors helps you develop a connection with the earth's natural frequency, increasing your sensitivity to energy flow and balance.

1. **Choose a Natural Setting**
   Go to a quiet place outdoors, such as a park or forest. Stand or sit in a comfortable position, barefoot if possible, and take a few deep breaths, letting yourself relax into the environment.

2. **Feel the Earth's Energy**
   Place your hands just above the ground, a plant, or a tree trunk. Focus on the energy you feel coming from the earth or plant—notice any warmth, coolness, or vibrational sensation that differs from man-made environments.

3. **Absorb and Reflect on the Sensation**

Allow yourself to absorb the earth's energy, visualizing it moving up through your feet and filling your body. Notice any calming or stabilizing effects, as well as any shifts in your energy field.

4. **Return to This Practice Regularly**

Spending time in nature strengthens your sensitivity to organic energy flows. Over time, you may start to pick up on natural energy flows more readily, which enhances your pendulum work by tuning you to earth energies and organic vibrations.

When I began working on my energy sensitivity, I initially found it challenging to pick up on subtle sensations. I sometimes doubted whether I was "doing it right" or if I was even sensitive enough to feel these shifts. But with consistency, my energy awareness grew stronger, and I began to notice sensations that were once too faint to register.

One of my breakthrough moments happened during the energy scanning exercise with objects. I held a smooth crystal in one hand and a piece of rough bark in the other. Closing my eyes, I felt the crystal's energy as calm and focused, while the bark felt raw and vibrant. I realized these sensations were my intuitive responses to each material's unique energy signature, confirming that I was becoming more attuned to subtle energies.

These exercises build not only energy sensitivity but also confidence in your intuitive abilities. By practicing regularly, you can refine your awareness of subtle energies, improving your pendulum work and enhancing your overall intuition.

Journaling and Tracking Pendulum Readings for Better Intuition

Journaling is a powerful tool for anyone working with pendulums, as it allows you to document your insights, progress, and patterns over time. By recording your pendulum readings and the experiences associated with them, you can identify trends, recognize moments of intuitive clarity, and improve your technique. A journal also serves as a valuable reference, helping you revisit previous readings and compare them to present situations. This section will guide you on how to set up a pendulum journal, what to track, and how regular journaling can enhance your intuition and effectiveness in pendulum work.

The Benefits of Journaling Your Pendulum Practice

When you first start working with a pendulum, your movements and insights may feel spontaneous or even unpredictable. By recording each reading, you gain a deeper understanding of how your pendulum communicates, as well as how external factors—such as your emotional state, location, or even the time of day—may influence your readings. Journaling provides several benefits for developing your intuition:

- **Enhanced Accuracy and Consistency**: Documenting each reading lets you analyze and track how your pendulum responds over time, creating consistency in interpreting its movements.

- **Noticing Patterns**: Tracking daily or weekly readings helps identify recurring patterns in your pendulum's movements, which may suggest a developing "language" between you and your pendulum.

- **Intuitive Development**: Reviewing your entries helps you recognize when your intuition was correct, building trust in your gut feelings and decisions.

- **Self-Reflection**: A journal allows you to reflect on your intentions and the emotional or energetic states present during each reading, which can lead to greater self-awareness and emotional growth.

How to Start a Pendulum Journal

Setting up a pendulum journal doesn't require any special format—any notebook, digital journal, or spreadsheet can work. However, using a structured approach can help you get the most out of your journaling practice. Below is a step-by-step guide to starting a pendulum journal.

Step 1: Choose a Medium

Decide whether you prefer to use physical or digital notebook for your journal. Physical journals offer a more tactile experience, while digital ones make it easier to search and analyze previous entries. Some people find it helpful to use both—a physical journal for everyday notes and a digital version for tracking patterns over time.

Step 2: Set Up a Standard Format

Consistency is key when journaling for pendulum work. Using a standard entry format makes it easier to spot trends and patterns. Here's an example layout:

- **Date and Time**: Make a note of when you did the reading. Certain times of day may influence how in tune you feel with your pendulum.
- **Question Asked**: Record the exact question you asked. Precise questions often yield clearer answers.
- **Response and Movements**: Describe the pendulum's movement (e.g., clockwise, counterclockwise, swinging vertically or horizontally).
- **Initial Interpretation**: Write down your interpretation of the response. Did you feel confident, unsure, or conflicted?
- **Emotional State**: Describe any emotions or physical sensations you experienced before or during the session, as these can impact your interpretation.

- **Outcome or Follow-Up**: If applicable, write any follow-up observations about whether the pendulum's response was accurate or relevant to the situation.

Step 3: Reflect and Summarize

At the end of each session, take a moment to write down any reflections or insights. What did you learn? Did anything stand out or feel particularly significant? This reflection phase is a valuable opportunity to build self-awareness and understanding of your intuitive growth.

Step 4: Review Regularly

Periodically reviewing your journal is crucial for seeing your progress. Once a week or month, look back over previous entries and see if any new insights or interpretations arise. This retrospective analysis can be incredibly validating as it allows you to see the gradual refinement of your intuitive skills and pendulum accuracy.

Sample Pendulum Journal Entry

Here's an example of a journal entry to illustrate how you might record your readings:

- **Date and Time**: November 12, 2024, 7:00 PM

- **Question Asked**: "Is it in my best interest to accept the new job offer?"
- **Response and Movements**: Pendulum moved clockwise in a strong, wide circle.
- **Initial Interpretation**: A clockwise movement generally indicates a positive answer, so I interpreted this as a "yes."
- **Emotional State**: Felt excited and a bit nervous about the possibility of a job change.
- **Outcome or Follow-Up**: I accepted the job and so far, it has aligned well with my goals.
- **Reflection**: This reading felt clear and confident. Looking back, I noticed that questions about career changes tend to produce strong responses, possibly due to my emotional investment in career choices.

By recording this information, you not only capture the pendulum's response but also allow space for personal insights that can add depth to your interpretations.

Tracking Trends in Pendulum Responses

Once you've maintained a pendulum journal for several weeks, you may notice patterns in how the pendulum responds to different types of questions. Here's how to identify trends and use them to strengthen your intuitive abilities:

1. **Review Questions and Consistent Answers**: Look back to see if similar questions have yielded consis-

tent responses. For instance, do questions about relationships produce certain movements or sensations?

2. **Identify Environmental Influences**: Documenting the time of day, moon phase, or emotional state might reveal environmental influences on pendulum accuracy. You may find that you receive clearer answers at certain times or during specific phases of the moon.

3. **Evaluate Interpretation Growth**: Over time, you may notice that your initial interpretations become more nuanced. Journaling helps track these changes, building confidence in your ability to interpret responses.

Enhancing Intuition Through Reflection

Reflection is one of the most powerful tools in intuitive development. Reviewing your journal entries allows you to learn from past experiences, recognize patterns, and observe how your intuition evolves. Here's how you can use reflection to deepen your intuition with pendulum practice:

1. **Reflect on Emotional Patterns**: Notice any recurring emotions or moods in your journal entries. Are there times when your pendulum readings seem more accurate or less reliable? Your emotional state may play a role in how well you connect with your pendulum.

2.   **Look for Synchronicities**: Pendulum readings often align with external events, revealing connections between your intentions and outcomes. Journaling lets you track these synchronicities, reinforcing your belief in your intuitive abilities.

3.   **Celebrate Your Progress**: Reviewing your journal regularly allows you to celebrate your growth. Acknowledging your development reinforces your commitment to pendulum practice, helping you stay motivated and attuned to your intuition.

Personal Reflection: Building Trust in Intuition

When I first started journaling my pendulum work, I found it challenging to commit to regular entries. However, once I began recording even small details, I noticed patterns emerging that I hadn't recognized before. For instance, my pendulum seemed to respond differently depending on my emotional state. Over time, I learned to recognize when I was too stressed to get a clear answer and began using grounding techniques before each session.

Through journaling, I also saw how my interpretations evolved. Entries that once seemed confusing became clear when I revisited them after a few months. This reflection helped me build confidence in my interpretations and recognize the importance of patience in developing intuitive skills.

Journaling and tracking your pendulum readings create a powerful foundation for intuitive growth. By consistently documenting your experiences, you can deepen your self-awareness, sharpen your interpretation skills, and build a personal record of your journey with pendulum healing. This practice transforms each pendulum session into an opportunity for learning, growth, and insight, helping you develop a more attuned, confident intuition.

Chapter 8: Practicl Applications and Case Studies

To fully appreciate the potential of pendulum healing, it helps to see real-world applications and hear from others who have had transformative experiences with this practice. In this chapter, we'll explore examples of pendulum healing in action through case studies, testimonials, and reflections from practitioners who have successfully used pendulums to facilitate healing for themselves and others. These stories offer insight into the profound effects that pendulum healing can have on physical, emotional, and spiritual well-being.

Real-Life Examples of Healing Sessions Using Pendulums

Case Study 1: Relieving Chronic Migraines
Lila, a holistic healer, worked with a client named Anna who suffered from chronic migraines for years. Anna had tried various treatments, from conventional medication to acupuncture, with only limited success. When she ap-

proached Lila for help, she was open to exploring new methods, including pendulum healing.

During their first session, Lila began by using her pendulum to scan Anna's energy field, focusing on identifying any imbalances in the chakras or surrounding energy field that might be contributing to her migraines. The pendulum swung in a wide, rapid circle over Anna's third eye chakra, which suggested an energy blockage in that area—often linked to headaches and issues of mental clarity.

Lila then used her pendulum for a balancing technique, visualizing energy moving through Anna's third eye chakra and releasing blockages while keeping the pendulum in a gentle, clockwise motion to encourage healing. After several sessions, Anna reported a significant reduction in both the frequency and intensity of her migraines. While the relief wasn't immediate, her migraines gradually decreased over time as the blocked energy around her third eye chakra was addressed and cleared.

This case highlights the potential of pendulum healing for working with chronic conditions, especially those related to energy blockages in specific areas. For Anna, the third eye chakra alignment appeared to be the key to reducing her migraines, demonstrating how targeted energy work can support healing.

Case Study 2: Releasing Emotional Trauma
Emotional trauma can manifest in the energy field as stag-

nant or blocked energy, leading to symptoms like anxiety, sadness, and even physical discomfort. Tom, an energy healer specializing in trauma recovery, worked with a client, Sarah, who experienced intense anxiety related to a past relationship. She was looking for a way to release these feelings without reliving the traumatic events, and pendulum healing offered a gentle approach.

In their first session, Tom used his pendulum to scan Sarah's heart chakra, which quickly revealed a blockage. The pendulum barely moved, indicating a constricted energy field, which is common in people dealing with unresolved grief or emotional trauma. To help open her heart chakra and allow a release of energy, Tom guided Sarah in a grounding visualization before using his pendulum to gently initiate energy flow in a clockwise direction.

As they worked together over several sessions, Tom incorporated affirmations and guided breathing exercises while using the pendulum to keep the heart chakra in balance. Sarah began feeling lighter and less emotionally burdened with each session. Over time, she reported a newfound sense of peace and no longer experienced the intense anxiety that once held her back.

Sarah's journey illustrates how pendulums can be instrumental in releasing long-held emotional traumas. By combining energy work with affirmations and breathwork, pendulum healing offered a non-invasive way for her to process and release painful emotions without reliving past traumas directly.

Testimonials and Experiences from Practitioners

Testimonial 1: Building Intuitive Trust Through Pendulum Healing

Julia, an experienced Reiki practitioner, added pendulum work to her practice to deepen her connection with clients and their energy fields. Initially, she found it challenging to interpret the pendulum's subtle movements, especially since she was more accustomed to the tactile nature of Reiki. However, as she continued working with her pendulum, Julia discovered that it was not only a tool for identifying blockages but also a way to confirm her intuitive feelings during sessions.

In her testimonial, Julia describes how the pendulum has helped her develop a stronger trust in her intuition: "Before using a pendulum, I doubted my instincts, especially when working with clients who were dealing with complex emotional issues. The pendulum has become a kind of 'third voice' in my sessions, offering confirmation for what I feel intuitively. This has helped me trust myself more and has improved the accuracy and impact of my energy work."

Julia's experience demonstrates the value of pendulums not just as tools for healing but also for building confidence in intuitive work. For many practitioners, the pendulum becomes a trusted partner, guiding them toward areas of concern and validating their inner knowledge.

Testimonial 2: Aiding Physical Healing with Pendulum Energy

Michael, a physical therapist with a passion for energy work, found himself increasingly interested in the holistic aspects of healing. He began experimenting with pendulums to support physical rehabilitation, especially for clients with persistent muscle pain that conventional therapy alone couldn't alleviate.

One of Michael's clients, James, had recurring knee pain from an old sports injury. Despite treatment, the pain persisted, and Michael sensed there might be an energetic component to the issue. Using his pendulum, he detected an energy blockage around the knee area and started incorporating pendulum healing into James's sessions.

Michael's pendulum work involved moving the pendulum in circles around James's knee, first to identify any energetic disturbances and then to "re-align" the energy flow in the area. After a few sessions, James noted a decrease in pain, which complemented the physical therapy he was receiving. "The pendulum," Michael shared, "added a new dimension to my practice. By addressing both the physical and energetic aspects of healing, my clients have experienced faster and more comprehensive recovery."

This testimonial highlights how pendulums can support physical healing by focusing on energy blocks that might contribute to lingering pain. Practitioners like Michael show that pendulums can serve as a bridge between conventional and holistic treatments, adding a layer of healing that addresses both body and energy field.

Testimonial 3: A Client's Perspective on the Emotional Benefits of Pendulum Healing

Linda, a client of pendulum healing, shared her experience after working with a practitioner who used pendulums to help her manage emotional stress and anxiety. "I was skeptical at first," Linda admits, "but after a few sessions, I started to feel a noticeable difference. It was as if a weight had lifted, especially after working on my throat and heart chakras. I never realized how much I'd been holding in, and the pendulum seemed to guide us exactly where the work was needed."

Linda's experience underscores how clients often respond to the targeted, personalized nature of pendulum healing. For Linda, the pendulum's movements over her heart and throat chakras revealed areas of emotional tension that might not have been addressed in other forms of healing. The process allowed her to become more aware of her emotional landscape and empowered her to release energy that had been weighing her down.

The Role of Pendulum Healing in Real-World Settings

These real-life examples and testimonials reveal the versatility and effectiveness of pendulum healing across various applications. Whether used to address physical pain, release emotional trauma, or support a client's mental well-being, pendulums provide unique insights that enrich the healing process. For practitioners, pendulums are more than just tools—they are guides that deepen the connection to a client's energy field and offer valuable information that can enhance other healing modalities.

The experiences shared in this chapter emphasize the importance of patience, practice, and open-mindedness in working with pendulums. Each case study and testimonial demonstrates that pendulum healing can be a profound addition to a healer's toolkit, bringing transformative results to clients with a wide range of needs.

Chapter 9: Troubleshooting FAQ

Common Issues and How to Resolve Them

The Pendulum Isn't Moving

- **Possible Causes**: A pendulum that doesn't respond is often related to low energy flow, stress, or a lack of grounding in the practitioner.

- **Solution**: Begin by grounding yourself with a brief meditation or breathing exercise. Holding the pendulum gently, take a few deep breaths and relax. If the pendulum still doesn't respond, cleanse it with sage, sound, or another method. Sometimes, a lack of movement is simply a cue to reset your energy and intention before continuing.

Inconsistent Movements

- **Possible Causes**: Inconsistent swings may indicate that your energy isn't focused or that the question is too complex or vague for the pendulum.

- **Solution**: Try to rephrase your question as simply as possible, focusing on one idea at a time. For example, instead of asking, "Is this job the best choice for my career and finances?" try asking separately about career growth, finances, and other factors. If inconsistency persists, check that you are in a calm, focused state; energy fluctuations due to mood or stress can affect pendulum responses.

Erratic or Unusually Fast Swings

- **Possible Causes**: This can be a sign of intense or chaotic energy either from the practitioner or the environment.

- **Solution**: Start by cleansing both the pendulum and yourself with grounding exercises. Then, ask a control question (e.g., "Show me a 'yes'") to see if the pendulum returns to its usual response pattern. If the energy continues to feel erratic, take a break and revisit your questions later in a calmer state.

Pendulum Moves Too Slowly

- **Possible Causes**: A slow or lethargic pendulum movement can be a sign that the practitioner is tired, distracted, or lacking focus.

- **Solution**: Take a short break to regain your focus. A quick energy-boosting practice like deep breathing, hand rubbing, or even a few minutes of walking can recharge your energy. Slow movement can also mean that the question being asked is challenging for your current energy state, so consider simplifying it or revisiting it when you feel more alert.

Pendulum Gives Contradictory Responses

- **Possible Causes**: Contradictory answers may reflect internal doubts, conflicted feelings about the question, or subconscious resistance.
- **Solution**: Start by taking a few moments to clarify your intentions and ensure that your mind is free of conflicting thoughts. Ground yourself and then ask clear "control questions" to re-establish the pendulum's "yes," "no," and "maybe" responses. This reset can help synchronize your energy with your pendulum and create a more focused connection.

Myths and Misconceptions About Pendulum Healing

Myth 1: The Pendulum Has a "Mind of Its Own"

Pendulums don't possess consciousness; rather, they respond to subtle energy cues from you, the practitioner. The pendulum is a reflection of your own energy field and intentions, making it a tool for tapping into your intuition rather than an independent "mind." The pendulum's movement is guided by the energy and focus you bring to the session, along with subconscious movements from your own energy field.

Myth 2: Pendulums Give "Fortune-Telling" Answers

Pendulums are not crystal balls or tools for predicting the future; instead, they offer insight into current energy states and probabilities. Pendulum healing and dowsing are best used for gaining insight and understanding, not predicting outcomes with certainty. For example, you might use the pendulum to check for energetic alignments regarding a decision, but the ultimate choice and its outcome are influenced by many other factors, including free will.

Myth 3: Pendulums Work for Everyone Immediately

Some people may find that they need time to build a connection with their pendulum before it responds accurately. This process can take time, and each person's experience is unique. Developing a relationship with the pendulum and learning to interpret subtle movements is part of the journey, so don't be discouraged if it doesn't feel intuitive right away. Consistent practice will increase your sensitivity and improve your results.

Myth 4: Only Certain Types of Pendulums Are "Effective"

The material, shape, and even appearance of a pendulum can influence your connection with it, but there's no "one-size-fits-all" or "better" type of pendulum. Some people resonate strongly with certain materials, like crystal or wood, while others may find metal or stone to be more responsive. Ultimately, the best pendulum is one that resonates with your energy, so allow yourself to experiment and explore what feels right.

When Your Pendulum Isn't Responding: Steps to Reconnect

When a pendulum stops responding, it's often due to temporary energy misalignments rather than any permanent issue. Here's a step-by-step approach to reconnecting:

1. **Cleanse the Pendulum**
   Pendulums can pick up energy from environments or emotions, so start by cleansing it to remove any unwanted or stagnant energy. You can cleanse it with sage, salt, sunlight, moonlight, or other preferred methods. A well-cleansed pendulum is more likely to respond accurately and sensitively.

2. **Reconnect with Your Intentions**
   Take a moment to center yourself, setting a clear and focused intention for the session. This can be as simple as stating, "I am here to connect with my highest good and seek clarity." When your mind is focused and calm, the pendulum is more likely to respond.

3. **Engage in a Grounding Exercise**
   Grounding exercises help to stabilize your energy, making it easier to connect with your pendulum. Try a few deep breaths, visualization, or even brief

meditation to align yourself with the present moment. Visualize yourself rooted to the earth and feeling calm, balanced, and clear.

4. **Ask Control Questions**
   Begin with questions that you know the answers to, like "Is my name [your name]?" or "Am I wearing [item of clothing]?" These control questions help re-establish the pendulum's base movements and remind you of its natural response patterns. If it answers these questions correctly, you'll know that your pendulum's connection is back on track.

5. **Ensure Your Energy is in a Receptive State**
   A receptive state is essential for clear readings. Check for any lingering emotional tension, mental distractions, or physical discomfort that might impact the pendulum's response. If you're feeling resistant or overly analytical, take a moment to release those feelings so that you can receive the pendulum's energy fully.

6. **Take a Break if Needed**
   Sometimes, a non-responsive pendulum is simply a sign that it's time to step away for a bit. If you're feeling frustrated or exhausted, give yourself a break and return to it later. Pendulum work is most effective when you feel relaxed, receptive, and open.

Practical Tips for Consistent Pendulum Connection

1. **Maintain a Regular Practice**
    Consistency helps build your relationship with the
    pendulum and enhances your sensitivity to its subtle
    movements. Practicing with it daily, even for a few
    minutes, can keep your connection strong.

2. **Hold the Pendulum Gently**
    Holding the pendulum too tightly can restrict its
    movement. A gentle grip allows it to swing freely
    and respond more accurately to your energy. Focus
    on allowing the pendulum to "flow" rather than try-
    ing to control it.

3. **Stay Open and Neutral**
    The pendulum's effectiveness depends on your abil-
    ity to remain neutral, without attachment to specific
    answers. Approach each session with an open mind,
    allowing the pendulum to reveal whatever answer
    aligns with your highest good.

This troubleshooting guide is designed to help you over-
come common obstacles in pendulum work while dis-
pelling any misconceptions that may interfere with your
practice. By understanding the nuances of pendulum responses and respecting the energy dynamics involved, you
can create a harmonious and insightful relationship with
your pendulum. When your pendulum isn't responding or

seems to give unclear answers, remember that these moments are often opportunities for reflection, grounding, and realignment rather than permanent roadblocks. With patience, practice, and openness, pendulum healing can become a reliable and transformative tool in your energy work journey.

Chapter 10: Final Thoughts and Next Steps

This chapter serves as a heartfelt conclusion to your journey through pendulum healing. As you've learned, pendulums are more than tools—they're extensions of your energy, intuition, and intent. Moving forward, allow yourself to deepen your practice, learn from additional resources, and experience the unfolding journey that pendulum work can bring to your life.

Encouragement to Continue Practicing

Pendulum healing is a practice that grows over time, deepening as you invest more of yourself into it. Just like any art or skill, pendulum work improves with consistent practice and dedication. Each time you use a pendulum, you strengthen your connection not only to the tool itself but also to the subtle energies around and within you. Through each swing and every answer, you're building confidence, honing intuition, and cultivating a greater understanding of the energy field that shapes your life.

Expect moments of clarity alongside moments of doubt. Both are equally valuable in shaping your skills. Trust that the more you practice, the easier it will become to interpret the pendulum's responses. In challenging moments, remind yourself that every practitioner faces these obstacles, and each one brings growth. The most significant strides often come when we embrace learning curves, staying patient with ourselves as we deepen this art.

Commit to exploring new ways to incorporate pendulum healing into your daily routine. Whether for energy checks, guidance on decisions, or simply grounding yourself, find ways to let the pendulum become a trusted part of your daily life.

Suggestions for Further Resources and Advanced Learning

For those ready to go deeper into pendulum healing, there are countless resources available to expand your understanding and practice. Here are some suggestions for advancing your knowledge:

- **Books and Guides on Pendulum Dowsing**
  Many experienced practitioners have published works that dive deeper into specific aspects of pendulum dowsing, from advanced techniques to cultural perspectives on pendulum healing. Look for books by authors who specialize in energy healing, dowsing, or esoteric sciences.

- **Courses and Workshops**
  Many healing centers and online platforms offer specialized courses in pendulum healing and energy

work. These courses often provide direct guidance, new exercises, and the chance to work with experienced mentors. Workshops, both online and in person, allow you to gain insights and interact with other practitioners

- **Related Practices**
  Pendulum healing is just one way to work with energy. Practices like Reiki, crystal healing, meditation, and energy clearing can complement your pendulum work and deepen your connection to energetic fields. Experimenting with these techniques will expand your toolkit, helping you discover which methods resonate most strongly.

- **Mentorship and Community**
  Joining a community of like-minded individuals can make your journey both easier and more enjoyable. Look for online groups, local meetups, or forums where you can discuss pendulum healing, ask questions, and share experiences. Consider seeking a mentor if possible—someone who has years of experience in energy work and can help guide you along your path.

Learning is a lifelong journey, and each new resource will add another layer of understanding and insight. Continue seeking knowledge, as there is always more to explore in the world of pendulum healing.

Inspirational Notes on Deepening One's Connection to Healing

As you conclude this book, know that pendulum healing is not just a technique but a doorway to a richer, more meaningful relationship with yourself and the energies that surround you. Pendulums are tools that empower us to listen more deeply, respond with sensitivity, and make choices from a place of clarity and intention.

Each swing of the pendulum offers an opportunity to connect with the unseen, to understand ourselves better, and to make choices that align with our highest path. In many ways, your pendulum is a mirror of your inner world—a guide that helps reveal both the energies and truths that you may not yet be able to see clearly with your own intuition.

As you deepen this journey, remember to embrace the mystery of energy healing. There are many aspects of energy work that may not seem logical or linear, and that's perfectly natural. Part of the magic of pendulum healing is allowing space for wonder and curiosity. Trust that as you open your heart and mind, you'll be met with guidance and insight that may surprise and inspire you.

Finally, let your pendulum practice remind you that healing is an ongoing process. Just as you might use a pendulum to clarify decisions or align energies, remember that healing is about progress, not perfection. Whether in times of clarity or confusion, joy or challenge, let your pendulum serve as a grounding force, helping you stay connected to your intentions, intuition, and inner wisdom.

Thank you for allowing this journey to unfold, and may your practice of pendulum healing bring you insight, peace, and connection. Embrace each swing of the pendulum as a step forward on your path of healing, growth, and discovery.